50 Garden to Table Recipes for Home

By: Kelly Johnson

Table of Contents

- Heirloom Tomato Salad with Basil
- Zucchini Noodle Stir-Fry
- Roasted Beet and Goat Cheese Salad
- Herb-Infused Lemon Chicken
- Fresh Corn and Black Bean Salsa
- Garden Vegetable Frittata
- Roasted Pepper and Eggplant Dip
- Cucumber and Dill Gazpacho
- Sweet Potato and Kale Hash
- Stuffed Bell Peppers
- Spinach and Feta Stuffed Mushrooms
- Grilled Eggplant with Garlic Yogurt Sauce
- Carrot and Celery Root Soup
- Herb-Potato Wedges
- Tomato Basil Pasta
- Grilled Vegetable Skewers
- Butternut Squash and Sage Risotto
- Spinach and Mushroom Quiche
- Green Bean Almondine
- Strawberry and Arugula Salad
- Roasted Garlic and Tomato Soup
- Zucchini Bread
- Chilled Cucumber Soup
- Roasted Sweet Potatoes with Rosemary
- Beet and Orange Salad
- Herb-Infused Salad Dressings
- Fresh Basil Pesto Pasta
- Stuffed Summer Squash
- Garden Fresh Salsa Verde
- Grilled Corn on the Cob with Lime Butter
- Radish and Chive Butter
- Baked Kale Chips
- Carrot Ginger Soup
- Eggplant Parmesan
- Tomato and Cucumber Gazpacho
- Summer Squash and Corn Chowder

- Mixed Herb Compound Butter
- Garden Lettuce Wraps
- Sweet Corn and Tomato Salad
- Roasted Asparagus with Lemon Zest
- Fennel and Orange Salad
- Cucumber Mint Salad
- Spaghetti Squash with Marinara Sauce
- Cherry Tomato Bruschetta
- Fresh Herb Rice Pilaf
- Pumpkin and Sage Pasta
- Tomato and Mozzarella Caprese
- Chilled Beet Soup
- Grilled Portobello Mushrooms with Balsamic Glaze
- Herb-Roasted Chicken with Root Vegetables

Heirloom Tomato Salad with Basil

Ingredients:

- **4-5 medium heirloom tomatoes** (various colors), sliced into wedges or chunks
- **1 small red onion**, thinly sliced
- **1 cucumber**, peeled, seeded, and sliced
- **1/4 cup fresh basil leaves**, plus extra for garnish
- **3 tablespoons extra-virgin olive oil**
- **2 tablespoons balsamic vinegar** (or red wine vinegar)
- **1 clove garlic**, minced
- **Salt and freshly ground black pepper**, to taste
- **1/4 teaspoon sea salt** (optional, for a finishing touch)
- **1 tablespoon capers** (optional, for added tang)

Instructions:

1. **Prepare the Vegetables:**
   - Wash and slice the heirloom tomatoes into wedges or chunks, keeping their different colors for visual appeal.
   - Thinly slice the red onion and peel and slice the cucumber.
2. **Make the Dressing:**
   - In a small bowl, whisk together the extra-virgin olive oil, balsamic vinegar, and minced garlic.
   - Season with salt and freshly ground black pepper to taste.
3. **Assemble the Salad:**
   - In a large mixing bowl, combine the tomatoes, red onion, and cucumber.
   - Tear the fresh basil leaves into smaller pieces and add them to the bowl.
4. **Dress the Salad:**
   - Pour the dressing over the vegetables and gently toss to coat all ingredients evenly.
   - If using capers, sprinkle them over the salad at this stage.
5. **Season and Garnish:**
   - Taste the salad and adjust seasoning with additional salt and pepper if needed.
   - Garnish with extra fresh basil leaves just before serving.
6. **Serve:**
   - Transfer the salad to a serving platter or individual bowls.
   - Serve immediately for the freshest taste or chill for about 15-20 minutes to enhance the flavors.

Notes:

- For a touch of sweetness, you can add a handful of cherry tomatoes or a drizzle of honey to the dressing.
- This salad pairs beautifully with grilled meats, seafood, or as a standalone light meal.

Enjoy your vibrant and refreshing Heirloom Tomato Salad with Basil!

Zucchini Noodle Stir-Fry

Ingredients:

- **3 medium zucchinis**, spiralized into noodles (or use a julienne peeler)
- **1 tablespoon sesame oil**
- **1 red bell pepper**, thinly sliced
- **1 cup snap peas** or snow peas
- **1 cup carrots**, julienned or thinly sliced
- **1/2 cup shiitake mushrooms**, sliced (or other mushrooms of choice)
- **2 cloves garlic**, minced
- **1 tablespoon fresh ginger**, minced
- **1/4 cup low-sodium soy sauce** (or tamari for gluten-free)
- **1 tablespoon rice vinegar**
- **1 tablespoon hoisin sauce** (optional for added sweetness)
- **1 teaspoon sriracha** (optional for heat)
- **1 tablespoon cornstarch** (optional, for thickening sauce)
- **2 green onions**, chopped
- **1 tablespoon sesame seeds** (for garnish)
- **Fresh cilantro** (optional, for garnish)

Instructions:

1. **Prepare the Zucchini Noodles:**
    - Spiralize the zucchinis into noodles or use a julienne peeler. Place them on a paper towel and lightly salt them to draw out excess moisture. Set aside.
2. **Prepare the Stir-Fry Sauce:**
    - In a small bowl, mix together the soy sauce, rice vinegar, hoisin sauce (if using), and sriracha (if using). If you prefer a thicker sauce, dissolve the cornstarch in a small amount of water and add it to the sauce mixture. Set aside.
3. **Cook the Vegetables:**
    - Heat the sesame oil in a large skillet or wok over medium-high heat.
    - Add the garlic and ginger, and sauté for about 30 seconds until fragrant.
    - Add the bell pepper, snap peas, carrots, and mushrooms. Stir-fry for 3-5 minutes, or until the vegetables are just tender but still crisp.
4. **Add the Zucchini Noodles:**
    - Add the zucchini noodles to the skillet. Stir gently to combine with the other vegetables. Cook for 2-3 minutes, until the zucchini noodles are heated through but still slightly crisp.
5. **Add the Sauce:**
    - Pour the prepared stir-fry sauce over the vegetables and noodles. Toss gently to ensure everything is evenly coated. If you used cornstarch, cook for an additional 1-2 minutes until the sauce thickens.
6. **Finish and Garnish:**
    - Remove from heat and stir in the chopped green onions.

- Transfer to serving dishes and garnish with sesame seeds and fresh cilantro, if desired.
7. **Serve:**
    - Enjoy immediately as a light and refreshing main dish or as a side with grilled chicken, tofu, or shrimp.

Notes:

- You can customize this stir-fry by adding other vegetables like broccoli, baby corn, or bok choy.
- For added protein, consider tossing in some cooked chicken, tofu, or shrimp.

Roasted Beet and Goat Cheese Salad

Ingredients:

- **4 medium beets**, peeled and trimmed
- **2 tablespoons olive oil**
- **Salt and freshly ground black pepper**, to taste
- **4 cups mixed greens** (such as arugula, spinach, and/or baby kale)
- **4 ounces goat cheese**, crumbled
- **1/4 cup toasted pecans** or walnuts
- **1/4 cup red onion**, thinly sliced
- **1/2 cup dried cranberries** or pomegranate seeds
- **2 tablespoons balsamic vinegar**
- **1 tablespoon honey**
- **1 tablespoon Dijon mustard**
- **2 tablespoons extra-virgin olive oil**
- **1 clove garlic**, minced

Instructions:

1. **Roast the Beets:**
    - Preheat the oven to 400°F (200°C).
    - Wrap each beet individually in aluminum foil and place them on a baking sheet.
    - Roast for 45-60 minutes, or until beets are tender when pierced with a fork.
    - Allow the beets to cool slightly before peeling. Once peeled, cut into wedges or slices.
2. **Prepare the Salad Dressing:**
    - In a small bowl, whisk together the balsamic vinegar, honey, Dijon mustard, extra-virgin olive oil, and minced garlic.
    - Season with salt and pepper to taste. Adjust sweetness or acidity as desired.
3. **Assemble the Salad:**
    - In a large salad bowl, toss the mixed greens with a little of the dressing.
    - Arrange the roasted beet slices on top of the greens.
    - Sprinkle the crumbled goat cheese, toasted pecans (or walnuts), red onion slices, and dried cranberries (or pomegranate seeds) over the salad.
4. **Dress and Serve:**
    - Drizzle the remaining dressing over the salad.
    - Gently toss to combine or serve with the dressing on the side.
    - Garnish with additional cracked black pepper if desired.

Notes:

- For added flavor, consider roasting the pecans in the oven for a few minutes until fragrant.
- The beets can be roasted ahead of time and stored in the refrigerator for up to 4 days.

Herb-Infused Lemon Chicken

Ingredients:

- **4 bone-in, skin-on chicken thighs** (or 4 boneless, skinless chicken breasts)
- **2 tablespoons olive oil**
- **2 lemons**, zested and juiced
- **4 cloves garlic**, minced
- **1 tablespoon fresh rosemary**, finely chopped (or 1 teaspoon dried rosemary)
- **1 tablespoon fresh thyme**, finely chopped (or 1 teaspoon dried thyme)
- **1 tablespoon fresh parsley**, finely chopped
- **1 teaspoon Dijon mustard**
- **1 teaspoon honey**
- **Salt and freshly ground black pepper**, to taste
- **1/2 cup low-sodium chicken broth**
- **1 tablespoon capers** (optional, for added brininess)
- **Lemon slices** and **additional fresh herbs** for garnish

Instructions:

1. **Marinate the Chicken:**
    - In a bowl, whisk together the olive oil, lemon zest, lemon juice, minced garlic, rosemary, thyme, parsley, Dijon mustard, honey, salt, and black pepper.
    - Place the chicken in a large resealable plastic bag or shallow dish and pour the marinade over it.
    - Seal the bag or cover the dish and refrigerate for at least 30 minutes, or up to 4 hours for more intense flavor.
2. **Preheat the Oven:**
    - Preheat your oven to 400°F (200°C).
3. **Sear the Chicken:**
    - Heat a large oven-safe skillet over medium-high heat.
    - Remove the chicken from the marinade, letting excess marinade drip off.
    - Add the chicken, skin-side down (or top-side down if using boneless), to the skillet and sear for 4-5 minutes, or until the skin is golden brown and crispy.
4. **Add the Broth and Bake:**
    - Flip the chicken and pour the chicken broth into the skillet. If using capers, add them to the skillet as well.
    - Transfer the skillet to the preheated oven and bake for 25-30 minutes, or until the chicken reaches an internal temperature of 165°F (74°C) and is cooked through.
5. **Garnish and Serve:**
    - Remove the skillet from the oven and let the chicken rest for 5 minutes before serving.
    - Garnish with lemon slices and additional fresh herbs if desired.
    - Serve with your choice of sides, such as roasted vegetables, rice, or a fresh salad.

Notes:

- If you prefer a lower-fat option, you can use boneless, skinless chicken breasts and skip the searing step. Instead, bake the chicken directly, but note that the texture may be slightly different.
- For added flavor, consider adding a splash of white wine to the broth before baking.

Fresh Corn and Black Bean Salsa

Ingredients:

- **2 cups fresh corn kernels** (about 3-4 ears of corn, or use frozen corn if fresh isn't available)
- **1 can (15 oz) black beans**, drained and rinsed
- **1 red bell pepper**, diced
- **1/2 red onion**, finely diced
- **1 cup cherry tomatoes**, halved or quartered
- **1 avocado**, diced
- **1/4 cup fresh cilantro**, chopped
- **1-2 limes**, juiced (to taste)
- **2 tablespoons extra-virgin olive oil**
- **1/2 teaspoon ground cumin**
- **1/4 teaspoon smoked paprika** (optional, for added depth of flavor)
- **Salt and freshly ground black pepper**, to taste

Instructions:

1. **Prepare the Corn:**
    - If using fresh corn, bring a pot of water to a boil and add the corn cobs. Boil for 3-5 minutes until tender. Remove from the pot and let cool slightly. Cut the kernels off the cobs and set aside.
    - If using frozen corn, thaw it by running it under warm water and then draining well.
2. **Mix the Ingredients:**
    - In a large bowl, combine the corn kernels, black beans, diced red bell pepper, finely diced red onion, halved cherry tomatoes, and diced avocado.
3. **Prepare the Dressing:**
    - In a small bowl, whisk together the lime juice, extra-virgin olive oil, ground cumin, smoked paprika (if using), salt, and black pepper.
4. **Combine and Toss:**
    - Pour the dressing over the salsa mixture and gently toss to combine everything evenly.
    - Stir in the chopped cilantro.
5. **Serve:**
    - Let the salsa sit for about 15-20 minutes to allow the flavors to meld. Serve with tortilla chips, as a topping for tacos or grilled meats, or as a side dish.

Notes:

- For a bit of heat, you can add finely chopped jalapeño or serrano pepper to the salsa.
- This salsa can be stored in the refrigerator for up to 3 days. However, it's best enjoyed fresh to maintain the texture of the avocado.

Garden Vegetable Frittata

Ingredients:

- **8 large eggs**
- **1/4 cup milk** (or cream for a richer texture)
- **1 tablespoon olive oil**
- **1 small onion**, diced
- **1 red bell pepper**, diced
- **1 cup zucchini**, diced
- **1 cup cherry tomatoes**, halved
- **1 cup fresh spinach** (or kale, chopped)
- **1/2 cup shredded cheese** (such as cheddar, feta, or goat cheese)
- **2 cloves garlic**, minced
- **1/2 teaspoon dried oregano** (or fresh if available)
- **Salt and freshly ground black pepper**, to taste
- **1 tablespoon fresh basil** or parsley, chopped (for garnish)

Instructions:

1. **Preheat the Oven:**
   - Preheat your oven to 375°F (190°C).
2. **Prepare the Vegetables:**
   - Heat the olive oil in a large, oven-safe skillet over medium heat.
   - Add the diced onion and cook for 2-3 minutes until softened.
   - Add the red bell pepper and zucchini. Cook for an additional 4-5 minutes until the vegetables are tender.
   - Stir in the cherry tomatoes, spinach, and minced garlic. Cook for 1-2 minutes until the spinach is wilted and the garlic is fragrant.
3. **Prepare the Egg Mixture:**
   - In a large bowl, whisk together the eggs, milk, dried oregano, salt, and pepper.
4. **Combine and Cook:**
   - Pour the egg mixture over the sautéed vegetables in the skillet. Stir gently to distribute the vegetables evenly.
   - Sprinkle the shredded cheese on top of the egg mixture.
5. **Bake the Frittata:**
   - Transfer the skillet to the preheated oven and bake for 20-25 minutes, or until the frittata is set and the top is lightly golden.
6. **Garnish and Serve:**
   - Let the frittata cool slightly before slicing. Garnish with fresh basil or parsley if desired.
   - Serve warm or at room temperature.

Notes:

- You can customize this frittata by adding cooked bacon, sausage, or different vegetables according to your preference.
- Leftovers can be stored in the refrigerator for up to 3 days and make a great make-ahead meal.

Roasted Pepper and Eggplant Dip

Ingredients:

- **2 large red bell peppers**
- **1 large eggplant**, peeled and diced
- **3 tablespoons olive oil**, divided
- **3 cloves garlic**, minced
- **1 tablespoon lemon juice**
- **1 teaspoon ground cumin**
- **1/2 teaspoon smoked paprika**
- **Salt and freshly ground black pepper**, to taste
- **2 tablespoons fresh parsley** or cilantro, chopped (for garnish)

Instructions:

1. **Roast the Peppers:**
    - Preheat your oven to 450°F (230°C).
    - Place the whole red bell peppers on a baking sheet and roast for 20-25 minutes, turning occasionally, until the skins are charred and blistered.
    - Remove the peppers from the oven and place them in a bowl. Cover with plastic wrap or a clean kitchen towel and let steam for 10 minutes. This helps to loosen the skins.
    - Peel off the skins, remove the seeds and stems, and chop the peppers.
2. **Roast the Eggplant:**
    - While the peppers are steaming, toss the diced eggplant with 2 tablespoons of olive oil, salt, and pepper.
    - Spread the eggplant on a separate baking sheet and roast for 20-25 minutes, or until tender and golden brown. Stir halfway through for even cooking.
3. **Prepare the Dip:**
    - In a large bowl, combine the roasted peppers, roasted eggplant, and minced garlic.
    - Use a food processor or blender to puree the mixture until smooth. You can also use an immersion blender directly in the bowl for a chunkier texture if preferred.
    - Stir in the lemon juice, ground cumin, smoked paprika, and additional salt and pepper to taste.
4. **Finish and Serve:**
    - Transfer the dip to a serving bowl and drizzle with the remaining 1 tablespoon of olive oil.
    - Garnish with fresh parsley or cilantro.
5. **Serving Suggestions:**
    - Serve the dip with pita bread, crackers, or fresh vegetable sticks.
    - It also makes a great accompaniment to grilled meats or as part of a mezze platter.

Notes:

- For added depth, you can mix in a tablespoon of tahini or yogurt.
- The dip can be made ahead and stored in the refrigerator for up to 5 days. It can also be frozen for up to 3 months; thaw before serving.

Cucumber and Dill Gazpacho

Ingredients:

- **4 cups cucumber**, peeled, seeded, and chopped
- **1 small onion**, finely chopped
- **2 cloves garlic**, minced
- **1 cup plain Greek yogurt** or sour cream
- **1/4 cup fresh dill**, chopped (plus extra for garnish)
- **2 tablespoons olive oil**
- **2 tablespoons lemon juice**
- **1 cup cold water** (adjust for desired consistency)
- **Salt and freshly ground black pepper**, to taste
- **1/2 cup cherry tomatoes**, halved (for garnish, optional)
- **1/4 cup thinly sliced radishes** (for garnish, optional)

Instructions:

1. **Blend the Ingredients:**
    - In a blender or food processor, combine the chopped cucumber, onion, garlic, Greek yogurt, dill, olive oil, and lemon juice.
    - Blend until smooth. If the mixture is too thick, gradually add cold water until you reach your desired consistency.
2. **Season the Gazpacho:**
    - Taste and season with salt and freshly ground black pepper. Adjust lemon juice or dill if needed.
3. **Chill:**
    - Transfer the gazpacho to a bowl or pitcher and refrigerate for at least 1-2 hours to allow the flavors to meld and the soup to chill thoroughly.
4. **Serve:**
    - Before serving, stir the gazpacho well. Pour into chilled bowls or glasses.
    - Garnish with halved cherry tomatoes, thinly sliced radishes, and extra dill if desired.

Notes:

- For a more pronounced dill flavor, add extra dill to taste.
- This gazpacho can be made a day in advance and stored in the refrigerator for up to 3 days.

Sweet Potato and Kale Hash

Ingredients:

- **2 large sweet potatoes**, peeled and diced
- **1 tablespoon olive oil**
- **1 small onion**, diced
- **1 red bell pepper**, diced
- **2 cloves garlic**, minced
- **2 cups fresh kale**, stems removed and chopped
- **1/2 teaspoon smoked paprika**
- **1/2 teaspoon ground cumin**
- **Salt and freshly ground black pepper**, to taste
- **2 tablespoons fresh parsley** or cilantro, chopped (for garnish)
- **1 tablespoon apple cider vinegar** or lemon juice (optional, for a tangy finish)

Instructions:

1. **Cook the Sweet Potatoes:**
    - Heat the olive oil in a large skillet over medium heat.
    - Add the diced sweet potatoes and cook for 10-12 minutes, stirring occasionally, until they begin to soften and brown.
2. **Add Vegetables:**
    - Add the diced onion and red bell pepper to the skillet. Cook for 5 minutes, or until the onion is translucent and the peppers are tender.
    - Stir in the minced garlic and cook for an additional 1-2 minutes until fragrant.
3. **Add Kale and Seasonings:**
    - Add the chopped kale to the skillet and cook for 3-4 minutes, or until wilted and tender.
    - Stir in the smoked paprika, ground cumin, salt, and black pepper. Cook for another 2 minutes, ensuring everything is well combined and heated through.
4. **Finish and Serve:**
    - If using, drizzle the apple cider vinegar or lemon juice over the hash for a tangy touch.
    - Garnish with fresh parsley or cilantro before serving.

Notes:

- For added protein, consider topping with a poached or fried egg.
- This hash can be served as a side dish or a main course and is excellent for meal prep.

Stuffed Bell Peppers

Ingredients:

- **4 large bell peppers** (any color)
- **1 tablespoon olive oil**
- **1 small onion**, diced
- **2 cloves garlic**, minced
- **1 cup cooked rice** (white, brown, or wild)
- **1 cup cooked ground beef**, turkey, or sausage (or use a plant-based substitute)
- **1 can (15 oz) diced tomatoes**, drained
- **1/2 cup frozen corn** or fresh corn kernels
- **1/2 cup black beans**, drained and rinsed (optional)
- **1 teaspoon ground cumin**
- **1 teaspoon paprika**
- **1/2 teaspoon dried oregano**
- **Salt and freshly ground black pepper**, to taste
- **1/2 cup shredded cheese** (cheddar, Monterey Jack, or your choice)
- **Fresh parsley** or cilantro, chopped (for garnish)

Instructions:

1. **Preheat the Oven:**
   - Preheat your oven to 375°F (190°C).
2. **Prepare the Bell Peppers:**
   - Slice the tops off the bell peppers and remove the seeds and membranes.
   - If needed, trim the bottom of the peppers slightly so they stand upright.
3. **Prepare the Filling:**
   - Heat the olive oil in a large skillet over medium heat.
   - Add the diced onion and cook for 3-4 minutes until softened.
   - Stir in the minced garlic and cook for an additional 1 minute until fragrant.
   - Add the cooked ground meat and cook for another 3-4 minutes, breaking it up with a spoon.
   - Stir in the cooked rice, diced tomatoes, corn, black beans (if using), cumin, paprika, oregano, salt, and pepper. Cook for 5 minutes, allowing the flavors to meld together.
4. **Stuff the Peppers:**
   - Spoon the filling mixture into each bell pepper, packing it in gently.
   - Place the stuffed peppers in a baking dish, standing upright. If the peppers are wobbly, you can use crumpled foil or parchment paper to stabilize them.
5. **Bake:**
   - Cover the baking dish with aluminum foil and bake for 30 minutes.
   - Remove the foil and sprinkle the shredded cheese on top of each pepper.
   - Bake for an additional 10-15 minutes, or until the peppers are tender and the cheese is melted and bubbly.

6. **Garnish and Serve:**
    - Remove from the oven and let cool slightly.
    - Garnish with fresh parsley or cilantro before serving.

Notes:

- For a vegetarian version, use a mix of beans and vegetables in place of the meat.
- You can also add chopped spinach, mushrooms, or zucchini to the filling for extra veggies.

Spinach and Feta Stuffed Mushrooms

Ingredients:

- 12 large button or cremini mushrooms
- 2 cups fresh spinach, chopped
- 1 cup feta cheese, crumbled
- 2 tablespoons olive oil
- 2 cloves garlic, minced
- 1/4 cup breadcrumbs (optional, for added texture)
- 1/4 teaspoon dried oregano
- 1/4 teaspoon dried thyme
- Salt and pepper to taste
- Fresh parsley, chopped (for garnish)

Instructions:

1. **Preheat Oven:** Preheat your oven to 375°F (190°C).
2. **Prepare Mushrooms:**
    - Gently clean the mushrooms with a damp paper towel.
    - Remove the stems and set the caps aside. Finely chop the stems for the stuffing mixture.
3. **Cook Spinach and Mushroom Stems:**
    - Heat the olive oil in a skillet over medium heat.
    - Add the chopped mushroom stems and cook for about 3-4 minutes until they release their moisture and start to brown.
    - Add the minced garlic and cook for another minute.
    - Add the chopped spinach and cook until wilted and most of the moisture has evaporated (about 2 minutes). Season with salt, pepper, oregano, and thyme.
4. **Mix Filling:**
    - Remove the skillet from heat and let the mixture cool slightly.
    - In a bowl, combine the cooked spinach mixture with the crumbled feta cheese. If you're using breadcrumbs, mix them in now. Adjust seasoning with salt and pepper as needed.
5. **Stuff Mushrooms:**
    - Place the mushroom caps on a baking sheet or in a baking dish.
    - Spoon the spinach and feta mixture into each mushroom cap, pressing down gently to pack the filling.
6. **Bake:**
    - Bake the stuffed mushrooms for 15-20 minutes, or until the mushrooms are tender and the filling is golden on top.
7. **Garnish and Serve:**
    - Garnish with chopped fresh parsley before serving.

These stuffed mushrooms are great for parties or as a special treat. Enjoy!

Grilled Eggplant with Garlic Yogurt Sauce

Ingredients:

For the Eggplant:

- 2 large eggplants
- 3 tablespoons olive oil
- Salt and pepper to taste
- 1 teaspoon smoked paprika (optional, for extra flavor)

For the Garlic Yogurt Sauce:

- 1 cup plain Greek yogurt
- 2 cloves garlic, minced
- 1 tablespoon lemon juice
- 1 tablespoon olive oil
- 1 tablespoon chopped fresh dill or parsley (optional)
- Salt and pepper to taste

Instructions:

1. **Prepare the Eggplant:**
    - Slice the eggplants into 1/2-inch thick rounds.
    - Sprinkle both sides of the slices with salt and let them sit in a colander for about 30 minutes. This helps to draw out excess moisture and reduce bitterness.
    - Rinse the salt off the eggplant slices and pat them dry with paper towels.
2. **Preheat the Grill:**
    - Preheat your grill to medium-high heat.
3. **Season the Eggplant:**
    - Brush both sides of the eggplant slices with olive oil.
    - Season with salt, pepper, and smoked paprika if using.
4. **Grill the Eggplant:**
    - Place the eggplant slices on the grill.
    - Grill for about 3-4 minutes per side, or until the eggplant is tender and has nice grill marks. The eggplant should be soft and cooked through.
5. **Prepare the Garlic Yogurt Sauce:**
    - While the eggplant is grilling, mix together the Greek yogurt, minced garlic, lemon juice, olive oil, and fresh dill or parsley (if using) in a bowl.
    - Season with salt and pepper to taste.
6. **Serve:**
    - Arrange the grilled eggplant slices on a platter.
    - Drizzle or serve with the garlic yogurt sauce on the side.
    - Garnish with additional fresh herbs if desired.

This dish is great as a side, a light main course, or even as a topping for a grain bowl. Enjoy!

Carrot and Celery Root Soup

Ingredients:

- 2 tablespoons olive oil
- 1 large onion, diced
- 2 cloves garlic, minced
- 1 pound carrots, peeled and sliced
- 1 pound celery root (celeriac), peeled and diced
- 4 cups vegetable or chicken broth
- 1 bay leaf
- 1/2 teaspoon ground cumin
- 1/2 teaspoon dried thyme
- Salt and pepper to taste
- 1/2 cup heavy cream or coconut milk (optional, for creaminess)
- Fresh parsley or chives, chopped (for garnish)

Instructions:

1. **Prepare Vegetables:**
   - Peel and slice the carrots.
   - Peel the celery root and cut it into 1-inch cubes.
2. **Sauté Aromatics:**
   - Heat the olive oil in a large pot over medium heat.
   - Add the diced onion and cook for about 5 minutes, until softened and translucent.
   - Add the minced garlic and cook for another 1-2 minutes, until fragrant.
3. **Cook the Vegetables:**
   - Add the sliced carrots and diced celery root to the pot.
   - Stir well to combine with the onions and garlic.
4. **Add Broth and Seasonings:**
   - Pour in the vegetable or chicken broth.
   - Add the bay leaf, ground cumin, dried thyme, salt, and pepper.
   - Bring the mixture to a boil, then reduce the heat to a simmer.
   - Cover and cook for about 20-25 minutes, or until the carrots and celery root are tender.
5. **Blend the Soup:**
   - Remove the bay leaf from the pot.
   - Use an immersion blender to puree the soup until smooth. Alternatively, you can transfer the soup in batches to a blender and blend until smooth, then return it to the pot.
6. **Add Creaminess (Optional):**
   - If you want a creamier soup, stir in the heavy cream or coconut milk.
   - Heat the soup gently until warmed through.
7. **Adjust Seasoning:**

        ◦ Taste the soup and adjust seasoning with additional salt and pepper if needed.
8. **Serve:**
        ◦ Ladle the soup into bowls.
        ◦ Garnish with fresh parsley or chives.

This soup is perfect on its own or paired with a crusty bread. Enjoy!

Herb-Potato Wedges

Ingredients:

- 4 medium russet potatoes (or any variety suitable for baking)
- 3 tablespoons olive oil
- 1 tablespoon fresh rosemary, chopped (or 1 teaspoon dried rosemary)
- 1 tablespoon fresh thyme, chopped (or 1 teaspoon dried thyme)
- 2 cloves garlic, minced
- 1 teaspoon paprika
- 1/2 teaspoon onion powder
- Salt and pepper to taste
- Optional: grated Parmesan cheese for extra flavor

Instructions:

1. **Preheat Oven:**
   - Preheat your oven to 425°F (220°C).
2. **Prepare Potatoes:**
   - Wash and scrub the potatoes thoroughly.
   - Cut each potato into wedges. You can do this by slicing the potato in half lengthwise, then slicing each half into wedges.
3. **Season Potatoes:**
   - In a large bowl, toss the potato wedges with olive oil, ensuring they are evenly coated.
   - Add the chopped rosemary, thyme, minced garlic, paprika, onion powder, salt, and pepper. Toss again until the potatoes are well-coated with the seasoning.
4. **Arrange for Baking:**
   - Spread the potato wedges out in a single layer on a baking sheet. For extra crispiness, use a rimmed baking sheet and make sure the wedges aren't overcrowded.
5. **Bake:**
   - Bake in the preheated oven for 30-35 minutes, or until the potato wedges are golden brown and crispy on the outside. Flip the wedges halfway through the baking time for even crisping.
6. **Optional - Add Parmesan:**
   - If desired, sprinkle grated Parmesan cheese over the wedges during the last 5 minutes of baking.
7. **Serve:**
   - Once the wedges are done, remove them from the oven and let them cool slightly before serving.
   - Garnish with additional fresh herbs if desired.

These herb-potato wedges are delicious on their own or served with your favorite dipping sauces like ketchup, aioli, or ranch dressing. Enjoy!

Tomato Basil Pasta

Ingredients:

- 12 oz (340g) pasta (spaghetti, penne, or your favorite type)
- 2 tablespoons olive oil
- 3 cloves garlic, minced
- 1 can (14.5 oz) crushed tomatoes or tomato sauce
- 1 can (6 oz) tomato paste (optional, for a richer sauce)
- 1 teaspoon dried oregano
- 1/2 teaspoon dried basil (or 1/4 cup fresh basil, chopped)
- Salt and pepper to taste
- 1/2 teaspoon sugar (optional, to balance acidity)
- 1/4 cup fresh basil leaves, chopped (for garnish)
- Freshly grated Parmesan cheese (for serving)

Instructions:

1. **Cook the Pasta:**
   - Cook the pasta according to package instructions until al dente. Drain and set aside.
2. **Prepare the Sauce:**
   - Heat olive oil in a large skillet over medium heat.
   - Add minced garlic and sauté for about 1 minute, until fragrant but not browned.
   - Stir in the crushed tomatoes and tomato paste (if using). Mix well.
3. **Season the Sauce:**
   - Add the dried oregano, dried basil, salt, pepper, and sugar (if using). Stir to combine.
   - Let the sauce simmer for about 10-15 minutes, stirring occasionally, until it thickens slightly and the flavors meld.
4. **Combine Pasta and Sauce:**
   - Add the cooked pasta to the skillet with the sauce. Toss well to coat the pasta evenly with the sauce.
5. **Add Fresh Basil:**
   - Stir in the fresh basil leaves. Cook for another 1-2 minutes until the basil is wilted and the pasta is heated through.
6. **Serve:**
   - Divide the pasta among serving plates.
   - Garnish with additional fresh basil and freshly grated Parmesan cheese.

This tomato basil pasta is delightful on its own or can be served with a side salad and crusty bread. Enjoy!

Grilled Vegetable Skewers

Ingredients:

- 1 red bell pepper
- 1 yellow bell pepper
- 1 zucchini
- 1 red onion
- 8 oz (225g) cherry tomatoes
- 8 oz (225g) mushrooms (button or cremini)
- 2 tablespoons olive oil
- 2 cloves garlic, minced
- 1 teaspoon dried oregano
- 1 teaspoon dried basil
- 1/2 teaspoon paprika
- Salt and pepper to taste
- Fresh herbs for garnish (optional, such as parsley or basil)

Instructions:

1. **Prepare the Vegetables:**
    - Cut the bell peppers into bite-sized chunks.
    - Slice the zucchini into thick rounds.
    - Cut the red onion into wedges.
    - Leave the cherry tomatoes and mushrooms whole.
2. **Make the Marinade:**
    - In a small bowl, combine the olive oil, minced garlic, dried oregano, dried basil, paprika, salt, and pepper. Mix well.
3. **Marinate the Vegetables:**
    - Place the chopped vegetables in a large bowl.
    - Pour the marinade over the vegetables and toss to coat evenly. Let them marinate for at least 15 minutes, or up to 30 minutes if you have time.
4. **Prepare the Skewers:**
    - If using wooden skewers, soak them in water for 30 minutes to prevent burning. If using metal skewers, you can skip this step.
    - Thread the vegetables onto the skewers, alternating between different types for variety. Leave a little space between each piece for even grilling.
5. **Grill the Skewers:**
    - Preheat your grill to medium-high heat.
    - Place the vegetable skewers on the grill and cook for about 10-15 minutes, turning occasionally, until the vegetables are tender and have nice grill marks.
6. **Serve:**
    - Remove the skewers from the grill.
    - Garnish with fresh herbs if desired and serve immediately.

These grilled vegetable skewers are delicious as a side dish, in wraps, or even on their own with a dipping sauce. Enjoy!

Butternut Squash and Sage Risotto

Ingredients:

- **For the Risotto:**
    - 1 small butternut squash (about 2 cups cubed)
    - 1 tablespoon olive oil
    - Salt and pepper to taste
    - 1 small onion, finely chopped
    - 2 cloves garlic, minced
    - 1 1/2 cups Arborio rice
    - 1/2 cup dry white wine
    - 4 cups vegetable or chicken broth (keep warm)
    - 1/2 cup freshly grated Parmesan cheese
    - 2 tablespoons unsalted butter
    - 1/4 cup fresh sage leaves, chopped (or 1 teaspoon dried sage)
- **For Garnish (Optional):**
    - Extra Parmesan cheese
    - Fresh sage leaves, lightly fried or crispy
    - A drizzle of olive oil

Instructions:

1. **Prepare the Butternut Squash:**
    - Preheat your oven to 400°F (200°C).
    - Peel, seed, and cube the butternut squash.
    - Toss the cubes with olive oil, salt, and pepper.
    - Spread them out on a baking sheet and roast for 25-30 minutes, or until tender and caramelized. Set aside.
2. **Cook the Risotto:**
    - Heat a large pan or skillet over medium heat and add a tablespoon of olive oil.
    - Sauté the chopped onion until translucent, about 5 minutes.
    - Add the minced garlic and cook for another 1 minute.
3. **Add the Rice:**
    - Stir in the Arborio rice and cook, stirring constantly, for about 2 minutes until the rice is lightly toasted.
4. **Deglaze with Wine:**
    - Pour in the white wine and stir until it's mostly absorbed.
5. **Add the Broth:**
    - Begin adding the warm broth one ladleful at a time, stirring frequently. Allow the rice to absorb most of the liquid before adding more broth.
    - Continue this process until the rice is creamy and al dente, which should take about 18-20 minutes.
6. **Incorporate the Squash and Sage:**

- Stir in the roasted butternut squash and chopped sage.
- Cook for an additional 2-3 minutes to heat through.

7. **Finish the Risotto:**
    - Remove the pan from heat and stir in the Parmesan cheese and butter until melted and well combined.
    - Season with additional salt and pepper to taste.
8. **Serve:**
    - Spoon the risotto onto plates or into bowls.
    - Garnish with extra Parmesan cheese, fresh sage leaves (crispy or fried if desired), and a drizzle of olive oil if you like.

This butternut squash and sage risotto is rich, creamy, and packed with flavor. It pairs beautifully with a simple green salad or can be served as a standalone dish. Enjoy!

Spinach and Mushroom Quiche

Ingredients:

For the Crust:

- 1 1/2 cups all-purpose flour
- 1/2 teaspoon salt
- 1/2 cup unsalted butter, cold and cut into cubes
- 2-3 tablespoons ice water

For the Filling:

- 1 tablespoon olive oil
- 1 cup mushrooms, sliced
- 2 cups fresh spinach, chopped
- 1 small onion, finely chopped
- 3 large eggs
- 1 cup heavy cream
- 1 cup milk
- 1 cup shredded cheese (such as cheddar, Swiss, or a blend)
- 1/4 teaspoon ground nutmeg (optional)
- Salt and pepper to taste

Instructions:

1. **Prepare the Crust:**
    - In a medium bowl, combine the flour and salt.
    - Cut in the cold butter using a pastry cutter or your fingers until the mixture resembles coarse crumbs.
    - Add ice water, one tablespoon at a time, mixing just until the dough comes together.
    - Form the dough into a disk, wrap it in plastic wrap, and refrigerate for at least 30 minutes.
2. **Preheat Oven:**
    - Preheat your oven to 375°F (190°C).
3. **Prepare the Filling:**
    - Heat olive oil in a skillet over medium heat.
    - Add the chopped onion and cook until softened, about 5 minutes.
    - Add the sliced mushrooms and cook until they release their moisture and start to brown, about 5 minutes more.
    - Stir in the chopped spinach and cook until wilted. Season with salt and pepper. Remove from heat and let cool slightly.
4. **Roll Out the Crust:**

- On a lightly floured surface, roll out the chilled dough to fit a 9-inch pie or quiche dish.
- Transfer the dough to the dish, pressing it into the bottom and up the sides. Trim any excess dough.
- Prick the bottom of the crust with a fork to prevent bubbling.
- Bake the crust for 10 minutes to set it slightly. Remove from the oven and set aside.

5. **Make the Quiche Filling:**
    - In a large bowl, whisk together the eggs, heavy cream, milk, and nutmeg (if using).
    - Stir in the shredded cheese and the cooked spinach and mushroom mixture.
    - Season with additional salt and pepper as needed.

6. **Assemble and Bake:**
    - Pour the filling into the pre-baked crust.
    - Bake for 35-45 minutes, or until the quiche is set in the center and the top is golden brown. A knife inserted into the center should come out clean.

7. **Cool and Serve:**
    - Let the quiche cool for a few minutes before slicing.
    - Serve warm or at room temperature.

This spinach and mushroom quiche is versatile and can be enjoyed on its own or with a side salad. It's also great for making ahead and storing in the fridge for easy meals throughout the week. Enjoy!

Green Bean Almondine

Ingredients:

- 1 pound fresh green beans, trimmed
- 2 tablespoons unsalted butter
- 1/4 cup sliced almonds
- 2 cloves garlic, minced
- 1 tablespoon lemon juice
- Salt and pepper to taste
- Lemon zest (optional, for garnish)
- Fresh parsley, chopped (optional, for garnish)

Instructions:

1. **Blanch the Green Beans:**
   - Bring a large pot of salted water to a boil.
   - Add the green beans and cook for about 3-4 minutes, until they are bright green and tender-crisp.
   - Immediately transfer the beans to a bowl of ice water to stop the cooking process. Let them cool for a few minutes, then drain and pat dry with a paper towel.
2. **Toast the Almonds:**
   - Heat a large skillet over medium heat.
   - Add the sliced almonds and cook, stirring frequently, until they are golden brown and fragrant. This should take about 2-3 minutes. Be careful not to burn them. Remove the almonds from the skillet and set aside.
3. **Cook the Green Beans:**
   - In the same skillet, melt the butter over medium heat.
   - Add the minced garlic and cook for about 1 minute, until fragrant but not browned.
   - Add the blanched green beans to the skillet and toss to coat them with the garlic and butter. Cook for about 2-3 minutes, just until heated through.
4. **Finish the Dish:**
   - Stir in the toasted almonds and lemon juice.
   - Season with salt and pepper to taste.
   - Cook for another minute, tossing gently to combine all the ingredients.
5. **Serve:**
   - Transfer the green beans to a serving dish.
   - Garnish with lemon zest and fresh parsley, if desired.

This green bean almondine pairs beautifully with a variety of main dishes, from roasted meats to fish. It's also a great side for holiday meals or any special occasion. Enjoy!

Strawberry and Arugula Salad

Ingredients:

- **For the Salad:**
    - 4 cups fresh arugula
    - 1 pint fresh strawberries, hulled and sliced
    - 1/4 cup crumbled goat cheese or feta cheese
    - 1/4 cup sliced almonds or walnuts (toasted if desired)
    - 1/4 red onion, thinly sliced (optional)
    - 1/2 avocado, sliced (optional)
- **For the Dressing:**
    - 3 tablespoons extra-virgin olive oil
    - 1 tablespoon balsamic vinegar (or red wine vinegar)
    - 1 tablespoon honey or maple syrup
    - 1 teaspoon Dijon mustard
    - Salt and pepper to taste

Instructions:

1. **Prepare the Dressing:**
    - In a small bowl or jar, whisk together the olive oil, balsamic vinegar, honey (or maple syrup), and Dijon mustard until well combined.
    - Season with salt and pepper to taste. Adjust the sweetness or acidity to your preference.
2. **Assemble the Salad:**
    - In a large salad bowl, combine the fresh arugula and sliced strawberries.
    - If using, add the sliced red onion and avocado.
3. **Add the Cheese and Nuts:**
    - Sprinkle the crumbled goat cheese (or feta) and sliced almonds (or walnuts) over the salad.
4. **Dress the Salad:**
    - Drizzle the dressing over the salad just before serving.
    - Gently toss the salad to combine, ensuring that the dressing is evenly distributed.
5. **Serve:**
    - Serve the salad immediately, or keep the components separate and combine them just before serving to prevent the arugula from wilting.

This strawberry and arugula salad is great on its own or as a side dish. It pairs well with grilled meats, seafood, or as a light lunch. Enjoy!

Roasted Garlic and Tomato Soup

Ingredients:

- **2 bulbs of garlic**
- **2 tablespoons olive oil**
- **1 onion, chopped**
- **1 carrot, peeled and chopped**
- **2 celery stalks, chopped**
- **1 can (28 oz) crushed tomatoes** (or about 5 cups of fresh tomatoes, peeled and chopped)
- **4 cups vegetable or chicken broth**
- **1 teaspoon dried basil**
- **1 teaspoon dried oregano**
- **1 bay leaf**
- **Salt and pepper to taste**
- **1 tablespoon sugar (optional, to balance acidity)**
- **1/4 cup heavy cream (optional, for creaminess)**
- **Fresh basil leaves for garnish (optional)**

Instructions:

1. **Roast the Garlic:**
    - Preheat your oven to 400°F (200°C).
    - Slice the tops off the garlic bulbs to expose the cloves.
    - Drizzle with a little olive oil, wrap in foil, and roast in the oven for about 30-35 minutes, or until the cloves are soft and caramelized.
    - Once roasted, let them cool slightly, then squeeze the garlic out of the skins. Set aside.
2. **Prepare the Soup Base:**
    - In a large pot, heat 2 tablespoons of olive oil over medium heat.
    - Add the chopped onion, carrot, and celery. Cook until the vegetables are softened and the onion is translucent, about 8-10 minutes.
3. **Add Tomatoes and Seasonings:**
    - Stir in the crushed tomatoes, roasted garlic (squeezed out of their skins), dried basil, oregano, and bay leaf.
    - Pour in the vegetable or chicken broth.
    - Bring the mixture to a boil, then reduce heat and let it simmer for about 20-25 minutes to let the flavors meld together.
4. **Blend the Soup:**
    - Remove the bay leaf.
    - Use an immersion blender to puree the soup until smooth. Alternatively, you can transfer the soup in batches to a blender, but be careful with hot liquids.
5. **Finish the Soup:**

- Taste and adjust seasoning with salt and pepper. If you prefer a slightly sweeter soup, stir in a tablespoon of sugar.
        - If you want a creamier texture, stir in the heavy cream.
6. **Serve:**
    - Ladle the soup into bowls.
    - Garnish with fresh basil leaves if desired.
7. **Enjoy:**
    - Serve hot with a slice of crusty bread or a grilled cheese sandwich for a comforting meal.

This roasted garlic and tomato soup is rich, flavorful, and perfect for a cozy night in. Enjoy!

Zucchini Bread

Ingredients:

- 1 1/2 cups all-purpose flour
- 1/2 teaspoon baking powder
- 1/2 teaspoon baking soda
- 1/2 teaspoon salt
- 1 teaspoon ground cinnamon
- 1/2 teaspoon ground nutmeg (optional)
- 1/2 cup unsalted butter, softened
- 1 cup granulated sugar
- 2 large eggs
- 1 teaspoon vanilla extract
- 1 cup grated zucchini (about 1 medium zucchini, unpeeled)
- 1/2 cup chopped nuts (walnuts or pecans), optional
- 1/2 cup raisins or chocolate chips, optional

Instructions:

1. **Preheat the Oven:**
   - Preheat your oven to 350°F (175°C). Grease and flour a 9x5-inch loaf pan or line it with parchment paper.
2. **Prepare the Zucchini:**
   - Grate the zucchini using a box grater or food processor. If the zucchini is particularly watery, you may want to squeeze out some of the excess moisture using a clean kitchen towel. You should have about 1 cup of grated zucchini.
3. **Mix Dry Ingredients:**
   - In a medium bowl, whisk together the flour, baking powder, baking soda, salt, cinnamon, and nutmeg (if using). Set aside.
4. **Cream Butter and Sugar:**
   - In a large bowl, using an electric mixer, beat the softened butter and sugar together until light and fluffy.
5. **Add Eggs and Vanilla:**
   - Add the eggs one at a time, beating well after each addition. Stir in the vanilla extract.
6. **Combine Ingredients:**
   - Gradually add the dry ingredients to the wet mixture, mixing just until combined.
   - Gently fold in the grated zucchini, and if you're using nuts, raisins, or chocolate chips, fold them in as well.
7. **Pour and Bake:**
   - Pour the batter into the prepared loaf pan and spread it out evenly.
   - Bake in the preheated oven for 60-70 minutes, or until a toothpick inserted into the center comes out clean.

8. **Cool and Serve:**
    - Allow the bread to cool in the pan for about 10 minutes before transferring it to a wire rack to cool completely.

This zucchini bread is perfect for breakfast, a snack, or even dessert. Enjoy it plain or with a pat of butter!

Chilled Cucumber Soup

Ingredients:

- 2 large cucumbers
- 1 tablespoon olive oil
- 1 small onion, chopped
- 2 cloves garlic, minced
- 2 cups vegetable or chicken broth
- 1 cup plain Greek yogurt or sour cream
- 2 tablespoons fresh dill, chopped (or 1 tablespoon dried dill)
- 1 tablespoon fresh lemon juice
- Salt and pepper to taste
- Fresh dill or chives for garnish (optional)

Instructions:

1. **Prepare the Cucumbers:**
   - Peel and seed the cucumbers. If you prefer a smoother texture, you can also peel the cucumbers entirely. Chop them into chunks.
2. **Sauté Onion and Garlic:**
   - In a medium-sized pot, heat the olive oil over medium heat.
   - Add the chopped onion and cook until it becomes translucent, about 5 minutes.
   - Add the minced garlic and cook for an additional minute, until fragrant.
3. **Cook the Cucumbers:**
   - Add the chopped cucumbers to the pot and pour in the vegetable or chicken broth.
   - Bring the mixture to a boil, then reduce the heat and simmer for about 10 minutes, until the cucumbers are tender.
4. **Blend the Soup:**
   - Let the soup cool slightly. Use an immersion blender to blend the soup until smooth. Alternatively, transfer the soup in batches to a blender.
5. **Add Dairy and Seasonings:**
   - Stir in the Greek yogurt or sour cream, fresh dill, and lemon juice.
   - Season with salt and pepper to taste.
6. **Chill the Soup:**
   - Cover the soup and refrigerate for at least 2 hours, or until it is thoroughly chilled.
7. **Serve:**
   - Ladle the chilled soup into bowls.
   - Garnish with additional fresh dill or chives if desired.
8. **Enjoy:**
   - Serve cold for a light and refreshing meal. It pairs well with crusty bread or a light salad.

This chilled cucumber soup is not only delicious but also very cooling and hydrating—perfect for a hot day!

Roasted Sweet Potatoes with Rosemary

Ingredients:

- **2 pounds sweet potatoes** (about 4 medium), peeled and cut into 1-inch cubes
- **3 tablespoons olive oil**
- **2-3 tablespoons fresh rosemary**, finely chopped (or 1-2 tablespoons dried rosemary)
- **Salt and pepper to taste**
- **1-2 cloves garlic, minced** (optional for extra flavor)
- **1 tablespoon honey or maple syrup** (optional, for added sweetness)

Instructions:

1. **Preheat the Oven:**
   - Preheat your oven to 400°F (200°C).
2. **Prepare the Sweet Potatoes:**
   - Peel and cut the sweet potatoes into 1-inch cubes. Try to keep the pieces roughly the same size for even roasting.
3. **Season the Potatoes:**
   - In a large bowl, toss the sweet potato cubes with olive oil, rosemary, salt, and pepper. If using garlic, add it to the bowl as well.
   - If you prefer a touch of sweetness, drizzle with honey or maple syrup and toss to combine.
4. **Roast:**
   - Spread the sweet potatoes in a single layer on a baking sheet. For best results, use a sheet pan with raised edges to prevent sticking and ensure even roasting.
   - Roast in the preheated oven for 25-30 minutes, turning halfway through, until the sweet potatoes are tender and caramelized. The edges should be slightly crispy.
5. **Serve:**
   - Remove from the oven and let cool for a few minutes before serving.
6. **Enjoy:**
   - Serve the roasted sweet potatoes warm as a side dish. They pair well with a variety of main courses, including roasted meats, grilled fish, or even a hearty salad.

This dish is not only flavorful but also healthy and versatile, making it a great addition to any meal!

Beet and Orange Salad

Ingredients:

- **4 medium beets**
- **2 large oranges**
- **1/4 red onion** (thinly sliced)
- **1/4 cup crumbled feta cheese** (optional)
- **2 tablespoons chopped fresh parsley** (or mint, if you prefer)
- **2 tablespoons extra-virgin olive oil**
- **1 tablespoon red wine vinegar** (or balsamic vinegar)
- **1 teaspoon honey** (or maple syrup)
- **Salt and pepper** to taste
- **A handful of mixed greens** (optional, for added texture and color)

Instructions:

1. **Prepare the Beets:**
    - Preheat your oven to 400°F (200°C).
    - Wash the beets thoroughly and trim the ends.
    - Wrap each beet individually in aluminum foil and place them on a baking sheet.
    - Roast for about 45-60 minutes, or until a knife or fork easily pierces through the beets. The cooking time may vary depending on the size of the beets.
    - Once cooked, let the beets cool slightly, then peel off the skins (they should come off easily). Slice or dice the beets into bite-sized pieces.
2. **Prepare the Oranges:**
    - While the beets are roasting, peel and segment the oranges. To do this, cut off the top and bottom of the orange so it sits flat. Use a knife to cut away the peel and pith, then cut between the membranes to release the segments. Alternatively, you can cut the orange into small chunks if you prefer.
3. **Make the Dressing:**
    - In a small bowl, whisk together the olive oil, red wine vinegar, honey, salt, and pepper.
4. **Assemble the Salad:**
    - In a large bowl, combine the roasted beets, orange segments, and red onion.
    - Drizzle with the dressing and gently toss to combine.
    - If using, sprinkle the salad with crumbled feta cheese and fresh parsley (or mint).
5. **Serve:**
    - Serve the salad on a bed of mixed greens if desired, or on its own.
    - Enjoy immediately, or let it sit for a bit to let the flavors meld together.

This salad is not only colorful but also a great balance of sweet, tangy, and savory flavors. It pairs well with grilled meats or can be enjoyed as a light, stand-alone meal.

Herb-Infused Salad Dressings

Ingredients:

- **1/4 cup extra-virgin olive oil**
- **2 tablespoons red wine vinegar** (or apple cider vinegar)
- **1 teaspoon Dijon mustard**
- **1 tablespoon fresh parsley** (finely chopped)
- **1 tablespoon fresh basil** (finely chopped)
- **1 clove garlic** (minced)
- **Salt and pepper** to taste

Instructions:

1. In a bowl, whisk together the vinegar, Dijon mustard, and minced garlic.
2. Gradually whisk in the olive oil until the dressing is emulsified.
3. Stir in the chopped parsley and basil.
4. Season with salt and pepper to taste.

2. Creamy Herb Dressing

Ingredients:

- **1/2 cup Greek yogurt**
- **1/4 cup mayonnaise**
- **2 tablespoons lemon juice**
- **1 tablespoon fresh dill** (finely chopped)
- **1 tablespoon fresh chives** (finely chopped)
- **1 clove garlic** (minced)
- **Salt and pepper** to taste

Instructions:

1. In a bowl, combine the Greek yogurt and mayonnaise.
2. Stir in the lemon juice, dill, chives, and minced garlic.
3. Season with salt and pepper to taste.

3. Lemon-Basil Dressing

Ingredients:

- **1/4 cup extra-virgin olive oil**
- **2 tablespoons fresh lemon juice**
- **1 tablespoon fresh basil** (finely chopped)
- **1 teaspoon honey** (or maple syrup)
- **1 clove garlic** (minced)

- **Salt and pepper** to taste

Instructions:

1. In a bowl, whisk together the lemon juice and honey.
2. Gradually whisk in the olive oil until the dressing is well combined.
3. Stir in the chopped basil and minced garlic.
4. Season with salt and pepper to taste.

4. Herb-Mustard Dressing

Ingredients:

- **1/4 cup extra-virgin olive oil**
- **2 tablespoons Dijon mustard**
- **1 tablespoon fresh tarragon** (finely chopped)
- **1 tablespoon fresh chives** (finely chopped)
- **1 tablespoon white wine vinegar**
- **1 teaspoon honey** (or maple syrup)
- **Salt and pepper** to taste

Instructions:

1. In a bowl, whisk together the Dijon mustard, white wine vinegar, and honey.
2. Gradually whisk in the olive oil until the dressing is emulsified.
3. Stir in the chopped tarragon and chives.
4. Season with salt and pepper to taste.

5. Mint-Lime Dressing

Ingredients:

- **1/4 cup extra-virgin olive oil**
- **2 tablespoons fresh lime juice**
- **1 tablespoon fresh mint** (finely chopped)
- **1 teaspoon honey** (or agave syrup)
- **1/2 teaspoon ground cumin** (optional)
- **Salt and pepper** to taste

Instructions:

1. In a bowl, whisk together the lime juice and honey.
2. Gradually whisk in the olive oil until well combined.
3. Stir in the chopped mint and ground cumin if using.
4. Season with salt and pepper to taste.

These dressings can be stored in an airtight container in the refrigerator for up to a week. Shake well before using to recombine the ingredients. Enjoy your herb-infused salads!

Fresh Basil Pesto Pasta

Ingredients:

- **12 ounces (340 grams) pasta** (such as spaghetti, penne, or fusilli)
- **2 cups fresh basil leaves** (packed)
- **1/2 cup pine nuts** (or walnuts as a substitute)
- **1/2 cup grated Parmesan cheese**
- **2-3 cloves garlic**
- **1/2 cup extra-virgin olive oil**
- **Juice of 1 lemon** (optional)
- **Salt and pepper** to taste
- **Cherry tomatoes** (optional, for garnish)
- **Additional grated Parmesan cheese** (for serving)

Instructions:

1. **Cook the Pasta:**
    - Bring a large pot of salted water to a boil.
    - Add the pasta and cook according to the package instructions until al dente.
    - Reserve about 1/2 cup of pasta cooking water, then drain the pasta.
2. **Make the Pesto:**
    - While the pasta is cooking, prepare the pesto. In a food processor or blender, combine the basil leaves, pine nuts, Parmesan cheese, and garlic.
    - Pulse until the ingredients are finely chopped.
    - With the processor running, slowly drizzle in the olive oil until the pesto reaches your desired consistency. You might need to scrape down the sides of the bowl occasionally.
    - Taste and adjust seasoning with salt and pepper. If you like, add a squeeze of lemon juice for extra brightness.
3. **Combine Pasta and Pesto:**
    - In a large bowl or the pot you used to cook the pasta, combine the drained pasta and pesto. Toss well to coat the pasta evenly. If the pesto is too thick, add a bit of the reserved pasta cooking water, a tablespoon at a time, until you reach the desired consistency.
4. **Serve:**
    - Serve the pasta warm, garnished with additional grated Parmesan cheese if desired.
    - Optionally, you can top with halved cherry tomatoes for added freshness and color.

Enjoy your fresh basil pesto pasta! It pairs wonderfully with a side salad and some crusty bread.

Stuffed Summer Squash

Ingredients:

- **4 medium summer squashes** (such as yellow squash or zucchini)
- **1 tablespoon olive oil**
- **1/2 cup onion** (finely chopped)
- **2 cloves garlic** (minced)
- **1/2 cup bell pepper** (finely chopped, any color)
- **1 cup cherry tomatoes** (diced or halved)
- **1 cup cooked quinoa** (or rice or couscous)
- **1/2 cup grated cheese** (such as Parmesan, mozzarella, or feta)
- **1/4 cup fresh basil** (chopped, or use parsley)
- **1/2 teaspoon dried oregano** (or Italian seasoning)
- **Salt and pepper** to taste
- **Optional: 1/4 cup pine nuts or chopped walnuts** (for added crunch)
- **Extra grated cheese** (for topping)

Instructions:

1. **Prepare the Squash:**
    - Preheat your oven to 375°F (190°C).
    - Wash the squash and cut off the ends.
    - Slice each squash in half lengthwise and scoop out the seeds and a bit of the flesh to create a hollow cavity. You can use a spoon or a melon baller to do this. Reserve the scooped-out flesh.
2. **Cook the Filling:**
    - Heat the olive oil in a skillet over medium heat.
    - Add the chopped onion and cook until softened, about 3-4 minutes.
    - Add the garlic and bell pepper, and cook for another 2 minutes.
    - Stir in the reserved squash flesh and cook until it's softened, about 3-4 minutes.
    - Add the cherry tomatoes and cook until they are softened and slightly blistered.
    - Stir in the cooked quinoa (or rice/couscous), cheese, fresh basil, dried oregano, salt, and pepper. If using, add the pine nuts or walnuts.
3. **Stuff the Squash:**
    - Place the hollowed-out squash halves on a baking dish or sheet.
    - Spoon the filling into each squash half, packing it in slightly.
    - Sprinkle extra grated cheese on top of each stuffed squash half.
4. **Bake:**
    - Bake in the preheated oven for 25-30 minutes, or until the squash is tender and the tops are golden and bubbly.
5. **Serve:**
    - Let the stuffed squash cool for a few minutes before serving.

Feel free to adjust the filling based on what you have available or your dietary preferences. For a vegetarian version, you can omit the cheese or use a dairy-free alternative. This dish makes a great side or a light main course!

Garden Fresh Salsa Verde

Ingredients:

- **8-10 tomatillos** (husks removed and rinsed)
- **1-2 jalapeño peppers** (seeded for less heat, optional)
- **1 small onion** (chopped)
- **2 cloves garlic** (minced)
- **1/2 cup fresh cilantro** (chopped)
- **Juice of 1 lime**
- **Salt** to taste
- **1 tablespoon olive oil** (optional, for a bit of richness)
- **1/2 cup water** (if needed, to adjust consistency)

Instructions:

1. **Roast or Boil the Tomatillos:**
    - **To Roast:** Preheat your oven to 425°F (220°C). Arrange the tomatillos and jalapeño peppers (if using) on a baking sheet. Roast for 15-20 minutes, or until the tomatillos are soft and have blackened spots.
    - **To Boil:** In a saucepan, cover the tomatillos and jalapeño peppers with water. Bring to a boil, then reduce heat and simmer for 5-7 minutes, or until the tomatillos are soft.
2. **Prepare the Salsa:**
    - If you roasted the tomatillos, let them cool slightly, then peel off the skins (if desired). If you boiled them, drain and let them cool.
    - In a blender or food processor, combine the tomatillos, jalapeño peppers, onion, garlic, and cilantro.
    - Blend until smooth. If the salsa is too thick, add a bit of water to reach your desired consistency.
3. **Season and Finish:**
    - Stir in the lime juice and salt to taste. If you like, add a tablespoon of olive oil for a touch of richness.
4. **Serve:**
    - Transfer the salsa verde to a bowl and let it sit for at least 30 minutes to allow the flavors to meld. Serve with tortilla chips, tacos, grilled meats, or as a topping for various dishes.

This salsa verde is a fresh and zesty addition to many meals and can be stored in the refrigerator for up to a week. Enjoy your homemade garden fresh salsa verde!

Grilled Corn on the Cob with Lime Butter

Ingredients:

- **4 ears of corn** (husks removed and silk cleaned)
- **4 tablespoons unsalted butter** (softened)
- **1 tablespoon fresh lime juice**
- **1 teaspoon lime zest**
- **1-2 cloves garlic** (minced, optional)
- **1/4 teaspoon chili powder** (optional, for a touch of spice)
- **Salt** to taste
- **Fresh cilantro** (chopped, for garnish, optional)

Instructions:

1. **Prepare the Corn:**
   - Preheat your grill to medium-high heat.
   - Remove the husks and silk from the corn. If you prefer, you can also soak the corn in water for 15-20 minutes before grilling to help keep it moist, but this is optional.
2. **Grill the Corn:**
   - Place the corn directly on the grill grates.
   - Grill the corn, turning occasionally, for about 10-15 minutes or until the corn is evenly charred and tender. You'll want to get a nice, even grill mark on the corn.
3. **Prepare the Lime Butter:**
   - In a small bowl, combine the softened butter, lime juice, lime zest, minced garlic (if using), and chili powder (if using).
   - Mix well until the ingredients are evenly incorporated. Season with salt to taste.
4. **Butter the Corn:**
   - Once the corn is grilled, remove it from the grill and brush it generously with the lime butter while it's still warm. You can also use a spatula to spread the butter evenly over the corn.
5. **Garnish and Serve:**
   - If desired, sprinkle the corn with chopped fresh cilantro for an extra burst of flavor and color.
   - Serve the corn immediately while it's hot.

This grilled corn on the cob with lime butter is perfect for summer barbecues and pairs well with a variety of dishes, from grilled meats to salads. Enjoy!

Radish and Chive Butter

Ingredients:

- **1/2 cup unsalted butter** (softened)
- **4-5 radishes** (finely grated or minced)
- **2 tablespoons fresh chives** (chopped)
- **1 clove garlic** (minced, optional)
- **1 tablespoon fresh lemon juice** (optional, for a bit of brightness)
- **Salt and pepper** to taste

Instructions:

1. **Prepare the Ingredients:**
    - Finely grate or mince the radishes. If you prefer a milder radish flavor, you can remove the radish tops before grating.
    - Chop the fresh chives finely.
    - If using, mince the garlic.
2. **Make the Butter:**
    - In a medium bowl, combine the softened butter, grated radishes, chopped chives, and minced garlic (if using).
    - Mix everything together until well combined.
3. **Season the Butter:**
    - Add salt and pepper to taste.
    - If you're using lemon juice, stir it in at this point to add a touch of brightness.
4. **Serve:**
    - Transfer the radish and chive butter to a serving dish or a small container.
    - It can be served immediately, but letting it sit in the refrigerator for a bit allows the flavors to meld together.
5. **Storage:**
    - Store any leftover butter in an airtight container in the refrigerator for up to a week. You can also freeze it for longer storage.

This radish and chive butter is perfect for spreading on crusty bread, serving with crackers, or using as a flavorful topping for roasted vegetables. Enjoy!

Baked Kale Chips

Ingredients:

- **1 bunch of kale** (about 6-8 cups of kale leaves)
- **1 tablespoon olive oil**
- **1/2 teaspoon salt** (or to taste)
- **Optional: 1/4 teaspoon garlic powder** (for extra flavor)
- **Optional: 1/4 teaspoon paprika** (for a smoky touch)
- **Optional: 1 tablespoon nutritional yeast** (for a cheesy flavor)

Instructions:

1. **Preheat Oven:**
   - Preheat your oven to 350°F (175°C).
2. **Prepare the Kale:**
   - Wash and thoroughly dry the kale. It's important that the kale is completely dry before baking to ensure it gets crispy.
   - Remove the kale leaves from the thick stems and tear them into bite-sized pieces.
3. **Season the Kale:**
   - Place the kale pieces in a large bowl.
   - Drizzle with olive oil and toss to coat evenly.
   - Sprinkle with salt, and any additional seasonings you're using (garlic powder, paprika, nutritional yeast), and toss again to distribute the seasonings.
4. **Arrange on Baking Sheet:**
   - Spread the kale pieces in a single layer on a baking sheet. Avoid overcrowding the pan; you may need to use two sheets or bake in batches.
5. **Bake:**
   - Bake in the preheated oven for 10-15 minutes, or until the kale is crispy and edges are slightly browned. Check frequently to prevent burning, as the kale can go from perfectly crisp to burnt quickly.
6. **Cool and Serve:**
   - Let the kale chips cool on the baking sheet for a few minutes. They will continue to crisp up as they cool.
   - Enjoy immediately or store in an airtight container for up to a week.

Feel free to experiment with different seasonings to suit your taste, like lemon zest, cayenne pepper, or even a bit of Parmesan cheese for added flavor. Enjoy your crunchy, homemade kale chips!

Carrot Ginger Soup

Ingredients:

- **1 tablespoon olive oil**
- **1 medium onion** (chopped)
- **3 cloves garlic** (minced)
- **1 tablespoon fresh ginger** (grated or minced)
- **1 pound (450 grams) carrots** (peeled and sliced)
- **4 cups vegetable broth** (or chicken broth)
- **1/2 cup coconut milk** (or heavy cream for a richer texture)
- **Salt and pepper** to taste
- **1/4 teaspoon ground cumin** (optional, for extra flavor)
- **1/4 teaspoon ground coriander** (optional)
- **Fresh cilantro** (for garnish, optional)
- **Lime wedges** (for serving, optional)

Instructions:

1. **Sauté the Aromatics:**
    - In a large pot, heat the olive oil over medium heat.
    - Add the chopped onion and cook until softened and translucent, about 5-7 minutes.
    - Add the minced garlic and grated ginger, and cook for another 1-2 minutes, stirring frequently.
2. **Cook the Carrots:**
    - Add the sliced carrots to the pot and stir to combine with the onion, garlic, and ginger.
    - Cook for 5 minutes, allowing the carrots to slightly caramelize.
3. **Add Broth and Simmer:**
    - Pour in the vegetable broth, and bring to a boil.
    - Reduce the heat and let it simmer for about 20 minutes, or until the carrots are tender.
4. **Blend the Soup:**
    - Using an immersion blender, blend the soup directly in the pot until smooth. Alternatively, you can blend the soup in batches using a countertop blender. Be cautious with hot liquids—let the soup cool slightly before blending if using a countertop blender.
    - If you prefer a chunkier texture, you can blend only half of the soup or use a potato masher for a rustic feel.
5. **Add Creaminess and Season:**
    - Stir in the coconut milk (or heavy cream) and season with salt, pepper, cumin, and coriander, if using.
    - Heat through, adjusting the seasoning to taste.
6. **Serve:**

- Ladle the soup into bowls and garnish with fresh cilantro and a squeeze of lime juice if desired.

This carrot ginger soup is delicious on its own or paired with a slice of crusty bread. It's also a great make-ahead dish, as the flavors deepen and improve after a day in the refrigerator. Enjoy!

Eggplant Parmesan

Ingredients:

- **2 medium eggplants** (sliced into 1/4-inch thick rounds)
- **Salt** (for drawing out moisture)
- **1 cup all-purpose flour**
- **2 large eggs**
- **1 cup breadcrumbs** (preferably Italian seasoned or panko for extra crunch)
- **1/2 cup grated Parmesan cheese** (plus extra for layering)
- **2 cups marinara sauce** (store-bought or homemade)
- **2 cups shredded mozzarella cheese**
- **1/4 cup chopped fresh basil** (optional, for garnish)
- **Olive oil** (for frying)

Instructions:

1. **Prepare the Eggplant:**
    - Preheat your oven to 375°F (190°C).
    - Arrange the eggplant slices in a single layer on a baking sheet or large plate. Sprinkle both sides generously with salt and let them sit for about 30 minutes. This step helps to draw out excess moisture and bitterness from the eggplant.
    - Rinse the eggplant slices under cold water and pat them dry with paper towels.
2. **Bread the Eggplant:**
    - Set up a breading station with three shallow dishes: one with flour, one with beaten eggs, and one with a mixture of breadcrumbs and 1/2 cup grated Parmesan cheese.
    - Dredge each eggplant slice in the flour, shaking off excess. Dip into the beaten eggs, then coat with the breadcrumb mixture, pressing lightly to adhere.
3. **Fry the Eggplant:**
    - Heat a few tablespoons of olive oil in a large skillet over medium heat. Fry the eggplant slices in batches until golden brown and crispy, about 2-3 minutes per side. Add more oil as needed between batches.
    - Place the fried eggplant slices on paper towels to drain excess oil.
4. **Assemble the Dish:**
    - Spread a thin layer of marinara sauce on the bottom of a 9x13-inch baking dish.
    - Arrange a layer of eggplant slices on top of the sauce.
    - Spread a portion of marinara sauce over the eggplant and sprinkle with mozzarella cheese and additional Parmesan cheese.
    - Repeat the layers until all the eggplant, sauce, and cheese are used, finishing with a layer of cheese on top.
5. **Bake:**
    - Cover the baking dish with aluminum foil and bake for 25 minutes.
    - Remove the foil and bake for an additional 10-15 minutes, or until the cheese is melted and bubbly and the top is golden brown.

6. **Garnish and Serve:**
    - Let the eggplant Parmesan cool for a few minutes before serving. Garnish with chopped fresh basil if desired.

This dish pairs wonderfully with a side salad or some crusty bread. It's perfect for making ahead of time and reheats well, making it a great option for meal prep. Enjoy your homemade Eggplant Parmesan!

Tomato and Cucumber Gazpacho

Ingredients:

- **4 cups ripe tomatoes** (chopped, or about 6 medium tomatoes)
- **1 large cucumber** (peeled, seeded, and chopped)
- **1 bell pepper** (red or green, chopped)
- **1 small red onion** (chopped)
- **2 cloves garlic** (minced)
- **1/4 cup extra-virgin olive oil**
- **2 tablespoons red wine vinegar** (or sherry vinegar)
- **1 cup tomato juice** (or vegetable broth for a lighter option)
- **1/2 teaspoon ground cumin** (optional)
- **Salt and pepper** to taste
- **1/4 cup fresh basil** (chopped, plus extra for garnish)
- **1/4 cup fresh parsley** (chopped, optional)
- **1/4 cup finely chopped cucumber and tomato** (for garnish, optional)

Instructions:

1. **Prepare the Vegetables:**
   - In a large bowl, combine the chopped tomatoes, cucumber, bell pepper, red onion, and garlic.
2. **Blend the Soup:**
   - Transfer the vegetable mixture to a blender or food processor.
   - Add the olive oil, red wine vinegar, and tomato juice (or vegetable broth). Blend until smooth. If you prefer a chunkier texture, blend until just combined, leaving some texture.
3. **Season and Adjust:**
   - Taste the gazpacho and season with ground cumin (if using), salt, and pepper.
   - Stir in the chopped basil and parsley if using.
4. **Chill:**
   - Transfer the soup to the refrigerator and chill for at least 2 hours to allow the flavors to meld and the soup to become cold.
5. **Garnish and Serve:**
   - Before serving, stir the gazpacho and adjust seasoning if needed.
   - Garnish with finely chopped cucumber and tomato, and additional basil if desired.

This gazpacho is perfect as a light lunch, appetizer, or refreshing snack. It pairs well with crusty bread or a light salad. Enjoy your chilled and flavorful tomato and cucumber gazpacho!

Summer Squash and Corn Chowder

Ingredients:

- **1 tablespoon olive oil**
- **1 medium onion** (chopped)
- **2 cloves garlic** (minced)
- **2 cups fresh or frozen corn kernels** (about 2 ears of corn if using fresh)
- **2 medium summer squash** (yellow squash or zucchini, diced)
- **1 medium potato** (peeled and diced)
- **4 cups vegetable broth** (or chicken broth)
- **1 cup whole milk** (or half-and-half for a richer chowder)
- **1/2 cup heavy cream** (optional, for extra creaminess)
- **1 teaspoon dried thyme** (or 1 tablespoon fresh thyme)
- **1/2 teaspoon paprika** (optional, for a touch of smokiness)
- **Salt and pepper** to taste
- **1/4 cup chopped fresh parsley** (for garnish, optional)
- **1/4 cup grated Parmesan cheese** (optional, for added richness)

Instructions:

1. **Sauté the Aromatics:**
    - In a large pot, heat the olive oil over medium heat.
    - Add the chopped onion and cook until softened and translucent, about 5-7 minutes.
    - Add the minced garlic and cook for another 1-2 minutes, stirring frequently.
2. **Cook the Vegetables:**
    - Add the diced potato and cook for 5 minutes, stirring occasionally.
    - Add the diced summer squash and cook for another 3-4 minutes.
3. **Add Broth and Corn:**
    - Pour in the vegetable broth and bring to a boil.
    - Reduce the heat and simmer until the potatoes are tender, about 10-15 minutes.
4. **Blend the Soup (Optional):**
    - For a creamier texture, you can use an immersion blender to partially or fully blend the soup. Alternatively, blend about half of the soup in a countertop blender and return it to the pot. This step is optional if you prefer a chunkier chowder.
5. **Add Corn and Dairy:**
    - Stir in the corn kernels, milk, and heavy cream (if using).
    - Add the dried thyme, paprika (if using), salt, and pepper.
    - Simmer for an additional 5-10 minutes, or until the corn is cooked through and the chowder has thickened slightly.
6. **Finish and Serve:**
    - Stir in the chopped parsley and grated Parmesan cheese (if using).
    - Adjust seasoning with salt and pepper if needed.

    - Serve hot, garnished with extra parsley or a sprinkle of Parmesan cheese if desired.

This chowder is delightful on its own or served with a side of crusty bread. It's a great way to enjoy the flavors of summer vegetables. Enjoy!

Mixed Herb Compound Butter

Ingredients:

- **1 cup unsalted butter** (softened)
- **2 tablespoons fresh parsley** (chopped)
- **2 tablespoons fresh chives** (chopped)
- **1 tablespoon fresh thyme** (chopped)
- **1 tablespoon fresh rosemary** (chopped)
- **2 cloves garlic** (minced)
- **1 teaspoon lemon zest** (optional, for a touch of brightness)
- **Salt and pepper** to taste

Instructions:

1. **Prepare the Herbs:**
   - Chop the fresh herbs finely to ensure they are evenly distributed throughout the butter.
2. **Mix the Ingredients:**
   - In a medium bowl, combine the softened butter, chopped herbs, minced garlic, and lemon zest (if using).
   - Mix well until all ingredients are thoroughly incorporated.
   - Season with salt and pepper to taste.
3. **Shape and Chill:**
   - Transfer the herb butter to a piece of parchment paper or plastic wrap.
   - Shape the butter into a log or a block, wrapping it tightly.
   - Chill in the refrigerator for at least 1 hour to firm up and allow the flavors to meld. For longer storage, you can freeze the butter.
4. **Serve:**
   - Slice or scoop the compound butter as needed. It can be used to top grilled meats, spread on bread, or melted over vegetables or pasta.
5. **Storage:**
   - Store the compound butter in the refrigerator for up to 2 weeks or in the freezer for up to 3 months.

Feel free to experiment with other herbs or add additional flavors like crushed red pepper flakes, minced shallots, or a splash of white wine. This herb butter is a fantastic way to enhance the flavor of many dishes with minimal effort. Enjoy!

Garden Lettuce Wraps

Ingredients:

- **1 head of butter lettuce, iceberg lettuce, or Romaine lettuce** (leaves separated and washed)
- **1 cup cooked quinoa** (or rice, for a heartier filling)
- **1 cup cherry tomatoes** (diced)
- **1 cup cucumber** (diced)
- **1 cup shredded carrots**
- **1/2 cup red bell pepper** (diced)
- **1/2 avocado** (sliced or diced)
- **1/4 cup red onion** (finely chopped, optional)
- **1/4 cup fresh herbs** (such as basil, cilantro, or mint, chopped)
- **1/4 cup crumbled feta cheese** (optional)

For the Dressing (optional):

- **2 tablespoons olive oil**
- **1 tablespoon lemon juice** (or red wine vinegar)
- **1 teaspoon Dijon mustard**
- **1 teaspoon honey** (or maple syrup)
- **Salt and pepper** to taste

Instructions:

1. **Prepare the Filling:**
    - In a large bowl, combine the cooked quinoa, cherry tomatoes, cucumber, shredded carrots, red bell pepper, and red onion (if using).
    - Gently fold in the avocado and fresh herbs.
2. **Make the Dressing (optional):**
    - In a small bowl or jar, whisk together the olive oil, lemon juice, Dijon mustard, and honey.
    - Season with salt and pepper to taste.
    - Pour the dressing over the vegetable mixture and toss gently to combine.
3. **Assemble the Wraps:**
    - Arrange the lettuce leaves on a serving platter.
    - Spoon the vegetable mixture into the center of each lettuce leaf.
    - Sprinkle with crumbled feta cheese if desired.
4. **Serve:**
    - Serve the lettuce wraps immediately, or keep the filling and lettuce leaves separate until ready to serve to avoid sogginess.

Variations:

- **Protein Add-ins:** Add cooked chicken, tofu, or shrimp to the vegetable mixture for extra protein.
- **Nuts and Seeds:** Sprinkle some toasted nuts or seeds (like sesame or sunflower seeds) on top for added crunch.
- **Sauces:** Serve with a side of soy sauce, hoisin sauce, or a spicy Sriracha mayo for extra flavor.

These garden lettuce wraps are refreshing, customizable, and make for a great light meal or appetizer. Enjoy creating your perfect wrap!

Sweet Corn and Tomato Salad

Ingredients:

- **2 cups fresh sweet corn kernels** (about 3-4 ears of corn, or use frozen corn, thawed)
- **2 cups cherry tomatoes** (halved or quartered)
- **1/2 red onion** (finely chopped)
- **1/4 cup fresh basil** (chopped)
- **1/4 cup fresh parsley** (chopped, optional)
- **1/4 cup crumbled feta cheese** (optional)
- **1 tablespoon olive oil**
- **1 tablespoon red wine vinegar** (or apple cider vinegar)
- **1 teaspoon honey** (or maple syrup)
- **Salt and pepper** to taste

Instructions:

1. **Cook the Corn:**
    - **Boil:** Bring a pot of salted water to a boil. Add the corn kernels and cook for about 3-4 minutes, or until tender. Drain and let cool.
    - **Grill:** Alternatively, you can grill the corn for a smoky flavor. Simply place the corn on a hot grill and cook for about 10 minutes, turning occasionally, until charred and tender. Remove from the grill and let cool slightly before cutting off the kernels.
2. **Prepare the Vegetables:**
    - In a large bowl, combine the cooked corn kernels, cherry tomatoes, and chopped red onion.
3. **Make the Dressing:**
    - In a small bowl, whisk together the olive oil, red wine vinegar, and honey.
    - Season with salt and pepper to taste.
4. **Combine and Toss:**
    - Pour the dressing over the corn and tomato mixture.
    - Gently toss to combine.
5. **Add Fresh Herbs and Cheese:**
    - Stir in the chopped basil and parsley (if using).
    - Sprinkle with crumbled feta cheese, if desired.
6. **Serve:**
    - Serve immediately or chill in the refrigerator for about 30 minutes to let the flavors meld.

This salad pairs wonderfully with grilled meats, seafood, or as a stand-alone light meal. It's perfect for picnics, potlucks, or a fresh side dish on a warm day. Enjoy your sweet corn and tomato salad!

Roasted Asparagus with Lemon Zest

Ingredients:

- **1 bunch of asparagus** (about 1 pound, trimmed)
- **2 tablespoons olive oil**
- **1 teaspoon lemon zest** (from about 1 lemon)
- **1 tablespoon fresh lemon juice** (optional, for extra zing)
- **2 cloves garlic** (minced, optional)
- **Salt and pepper** to taste
- **1 tablespoon freshly grated Parmesan cheese** (optional, for a touch of richness)
- **Fresh herbs** (such as parsley or thyme, for garnish, optional)

Instructions:

1. **Preheat Oven:**
    - Preheat your oven to 425°F (220°C).
2. **Prepare the Asparagus:**
    - Rinse the asparagus and trim the woody ends. To trim, gently bend each spear until it snaps at the natural break point, or cut off the tough ends with a knife.
3. **Season the Asparagus:**
    - Place the asparagus on a baking sheet.
    - Drizzle with olive oil and toss to coat evenly.
    - Spread the asparagus in a single layer on the baking sheet.
4. **Add Flavorings:**
    - If using, sprinkle the minced garlic over the asparagus.
    - Season with salt and pepper to taste.
5. **Roast:**
    - Roast in the preheated oven for 12-15 minutes, or until the asparagus is tender and slightly crispy on the edges. The cooking time may vary depending on the thickness of the asparagus spears.
6. **Finish with Lemon:**
    - Remove the asparagus from the oven and immediately sprinkle with lemon zest.
    - If using, drizzle with fresh lemon juice and toss gently to combine.
    - Optionally, sprinkle with freshly grated Parmesan cheese for added flavor.
7. **Garnish and Serve:**
    - Garnish with fresh herbs if desired.
    - Serve warm as a side dish to complement your main course.

This roasted asparagus with lemon zest is a versatile side dish that pairs well with a variety of entrees, from grilled meats to fish and pasta. Enjoy the bright, fresh flavors!

Fennel and Orange Salad

Ingredients:

- **1 large bulb of fennel** (trimmed and thinly sliced)
- **2 large oranges** (peeled and segmented)
- **1/4 red onion** (thinly sliced, optional)
- **2 tablespoons fresh parsley** (chopped, optional)
- **1/4 cup Kalamata olives** (pitted and sliced, optional)
- **1 tablespoon extra-virgin olive oil**
- **1 tablespoon white wine vinegar** (or apple cider vinegar)
- **1 teaspoon honey** (or maple syrup, optional for sweetness)
- **Salt and pepper** to taste
- **1/4 cup crumbled feta cheese** (optional)

Instructions:

1. **Prepare the Fennel:**
    - Trim the fennel bulb, removing the stalks and fronds. Save some fronds for garnish if desired.
    - Thinly slice the fennel bulb using a mandoline or a sharp knife.
2. **Prepare the Oranges:**
    - Peel the oranges and cut away any remaining pith.
    - Segment the oranges by cutting between the membranes to release the individual segments.
3. **Assemble the Salad:**
    - In a large bowl, combine the sliced fennel, orange segments, and red onion (if using).
    - If adding olives, mix them in.
4. **Make the Dressing:**
    - In a small bowl or jar, whisk together the olive oil, white wine vinegar, and honey (if using).
    - Season with salt and pepper to taste.
5. **Dress the Salad:**
    - Pour the dressing over the fennel and orange mixture.
    - Toss gently to combine, ensuring the fennel and orange are evenly coated with the dressing.
6. **Garnish and Serve:**
    - Garnish with chopped fresh parsley and fennel fronds if desired.
    - Sprinkle with crumbled feta cheese if using.
    - Serve immediately or chill in the refrigerator for 15-30 minutes to let the flavors meld.

This fennel and orange salad is a delightful combination of flavors and textures, with the crisp fennel complementing the juicy, sweet oranges. It pairs well with a variety of dishes, making it a versatile addition to your meal repertoire. Enjoy!

Cucumber Mint Salad

Ingredients:

- **2 large cucumbers** (peeled if desired, and thinly sliced)
- **1/4 cup fresh mint leaves** (chopped, plus extra for garnish)
- **1/4 red onion** (thinly sliced, optional)
- **1 tablespoon extra-virgin olive oil**
- **1 tablespoon lemon juice** (or white wine vinegar)
- **1 teaspoon honey** (or maple syrup, optional for a touch of sweetness)
- **Salt and pepper** to taste
- **1/4 cup crumbled feta cheese** (optional, for added flavor)

Instructions:

1. **Prepare the Cucumbers:**
    - Slice the cucumbers thinly using a knife or mandoline.
    - If the cucumbers have a lot of seeds or you prefer a milder flavor, you can scoop out the seeds with a spoon.
2. **Prepare the Mint:**
    - Chop the fresh mint leaves finely. Reserve a few whole leaves for garnish if desired.
3. **Combine Ingredients:**
    - In a large bowl, combine the sliced cucumbers, chopped mint, and red onion (if using).
4. **Make the Dressing:**
    - In a small bowl or jar, whisk together the olive oil, lemon juice (or vinegar), and honey (if using).
    - Season with salt and pepper to taste.
5. **Dress the Salad:**
    - Pour the dressing over the cucumber and mint mixture.
    - Toss gently to coat the cucumbers evenly with the dressing.
6. **Garnish and Serve:**
    - Garnish with extra mint leaves and crumbled feta cheese if using.
    - Serve immediately or chill in the refrigerator for 15-30 minutes to let the flavors meld.

This cucumber mint salad is crisp and refreshing, making it an ideal choice for hot days or as a light side dish. The mint adds a burst of freshness, while the lemon juice and honey balance the flavors beautifully. Enjoy your salad!

Spaghetti Squash with Marinara Sauce

Ingredients:

- **1 medium spaghetti squash**
- **2 cups marinara sauce** (store-bought or homemade)
- **1 tablespoon olive oil**
- **2 cloves garlic** (minced)
- **1/4 teaspoon dried oregano** (optional)
- **1/4 teaspoon dried basil** (optional)
- **Salt and pepper** to taste
- **1/4 cup grated Parmesan cheese** (optional, for serving)
- **Fresh basil or parsley** (chopped, for garnish, optional)

Instructions:

1. **Prepare the Spaghetti Squash:**
   - Preheat your oven to 400°F (200°C).
   - Cut the spaghetti squash in half lengthwise and scoop out the seeds with a spoon.
   - Drizzle the inside of each half with olive oil and season with salt and pepper.
   - Place the squash halves cut-side down on a baking sheet lined with parchment paper or foil.
2. **Roast the Squash:**
   - Roast in the preheated oven for 40-45 minutes, or until the flesh is tender and can be easily shredded with a fork. The cooking time may vary depending on the size of the squash.
   - Once done, let the squash cool slightly. Using a fork, scrape the flesh to create "spaghetti" strands. Set aside.
3. **Prepare the Marinara Sauce:**
   - While the squash is roasting, heat the olive oil in a saucepan over medium heat.
   - Add the minced garlic and cook for 1-2 minutes, until fragrant.
   - Add the marinara sauce, dried oregano, and dried basil (if using). Simmer for 10-15 minutes to allow the flavors to meld. Season with salt and pepper to taste.
4. **Combine and Serve:**
   - Toss the spaghetti squash strands with the marinara sauce in the saucepan, or serve the sauce on top of the squash.
   - Garnish with grated Parmesan cheese and fresh basil or parsley if desired.

This dish is versatile and can be customized with additional toppings such as sautéed mushrooms, roasted vegetables, or a sprinkle of red pepper flakes for a bit of heat. Enjoy your healthy and comforting spaghetti squash with marinara sauce!

Cherry Tomato Bruschetta

Ingredients:

- **1 pint cherry tomatoes** (halved)
- **1/4 cup fresh basil** (chopped)
- **1-2 cloves garlic** (minced)
- **2 tablespoons extra-virgin olive oil**
- **1 tablespoon balsamic vinegar** (optional, for a tangy touch)
- **Salt and pepper** to taste
- **1 baguette** (or crusty Italian bread)
- **1 clove garlic** (whole, for rubbing on toasted bread)
- **1/4 cup grated Parmesan cheese** (optional, for added flavor)

Instructions:

1. **Prepare the Tomato Mixture:**
    - In a medium bowl, combine the halved cherry tomatoes, chopped basil, and minced garlic.
    - Drizzle with olive oil and balsamic vinegar (if using).
    - Season with salt and pepper to taste.
    - Toss gently to mix everything together. Let the mixture sit for at least 15 minutes to allow the flavors to meld.
2. **Prepare the Bread:**
    - Preheat your oven to 400°F (200°C).
    - Slice the baguette or Italian bread into 1/2-inch thick slices.
    - Arrange the slices in a single layer on a baking sheet.
3. **Toast the Bread:**
    - Toast the bread slices in the preheated oven for about 5-7 minutes, or until they are golden and crispy. You can also use a grill or toaster for this step.
    - Once toasted, remove from the oven and immediately rub one side of each slice with a whole garlic clove for extra flavor.
4. **Assemble the Bruschetta:**
    - Spoon the tomato mixture onto the toasted side of each bread slice.
    - If desired, sprinkle with grated Parmesan cheese for added richness.
5. **Serve:**
    - Arrange the bruschetta on a serving platter and enjoy immediately while the bread is still crisp.

This cherry tomato bruschetta is perfect as an appetizer, snack, or even a light lunch. The freshness of the tomatoes and basil combined with the crispy bread makes for a delightful treat. Enjoy!

Fresh Herb Rice Pilaf

Ingredients:

- **1 cup long-grain white rice** (or jasmine rice)
- **2 tablespoons olive oil or butter**
- **1 small onion** (finely chopped)
- **2 cloves garlic** (minced)
- **2 cups chicken or vegetable broth**
- **1/2 cup fresh parsley** (chopped)
- **1/4 cup fresh basil** (chopped)
- **1 tablespoon fresh thyme** (chopped)
- **1 tablespoon fresh chives** (chopped, optional)
- **Salt and pepper** to taste
- **1/4 cup toasted pine nuts** or slivered almonds (optional, for garnish)

Instructions:

1. **Sauté the Aromatics:**
    - Heat the olive oil or butter in a medium saucepan over medium heat.
    - Add the chopped onion and cook until softened and translucent, about 5 minutes.
    - Add the minced garlic and cook for another 1-2 minutes, until fragrant.
2. **Cook the Rice:**
    - Add the rice to the saucepan and stir to coat the grains with the oil and aromatics.
    - Cook for 1-2 minutes, stirring occasionally, until the rice becomes slightly translucent.
3. **Add the Broth:**
    - Pour in the chicken or vegetable broth and bring to a boil.
    - Reduce the heat to low, cover the saucepan, and simmer for 15-18 minutes, or until the rice is tender and the liquid is absorbed.
4. **Add Fresh Herbs:**
    - Remove the saucepan from heat and let it sit, covered, for 5 minutes.
    - Fluff the rice with a fork and stir in the chopped fresh herbs (parsley, basil, thyme, and chives if using).
5. **Season and Serve:**
    - Season with salt and pepper to taste.
    - If desired, garnish with toasted pine nuts or slivered almonds for added texture and flavor.
6. **Serve:**
    - Transfer the rice pilaf to a serving dish and serve warm.

This fresh herb rice pilaf is a versatile side dish that pairs well with a variety of main courses, from roasted chicken and grilled fish to vegetable stir-fries and more. The fresh herbs elevate the flavor of the rice, making it a standout component of your meal. Enjoy!

Pumpkin and Sage Pasta

Ingredients:

- **12 ounces (340 grams) pasta** (such as penne, farfalle, or fettuccine)
- **1 tablespoon olive oil**
- **1 small onion** (finely chopped)
- **2 cloves garlic** (minced)
- **1 cup canned pumpkin puree** (or roasted pumpkin puree)
- **1/2 cup vegetable broth** (or chicken broth)
- **1/2 cup heavy cream** (or milk for a lighter version)
- **1/4 cup grated Parmesan cheese** (plus extra for serving)
- **1 tablespoon fresh sage** (chopped, or 1 teaspoon dried sage)
- **Salt and pepper** to taste
- **1/4 teaspoon ground nutmeg** (optional, for added warmth)
- **1 tablespoon unsalted butter** (optional, for extra richness)

Instructions:

1. **Cook the Pasta:**
   - Cook the pasta according to package instructions until al dente. Drain and set aside.
2. **Prepare the Sauce:**
   - In a large skillet or saucepan, heat the olive oil over medium heat.
   - Add the chopped onion and cook until softened and translucent, about 5 minutes.
   - Add the minced garlic and cook for an additional 1-2 minutes, until fragrant.
3. **Add the Pumpkin:**
   - Stir in the pumpkin puree and cook for 2-3 minutes to warm it through.
   - Add the vegetable broth and bring to a simmer. Cook for about 5 minutes to allow the flavors to combine.
4. **Finish the Sauce:**
   - Reduce the heat to low and stir in the heavy cream. If using, add the unsalted butter and stir until melted and combined.
   - Stir in the chopped sage (or dried sage) and grated Parmesan cheese.
   - Season with salt, pepper, and ground nutmeg (if using) to taste.
5. **Combine Pasta and Sauce:**
   - Add the cooked pasta to the sauce and toss to coat the pasta evenly.
   - Cook for another 2-3 minutes, or until everything is heated through and the pasta is well coated with the sauce.
6. **Serve:**
   - Divide the pasta among serving plates.
   - Garnish with additional grated Parmesan cheese and a few fresh sage leaves if desired.

This pumpkin and sage pasta is a comforting, rich dish with a lovely balance of flavors. It pairs well with a simple green salad and some crusty bread for a complete meal. Enjoy your seasonal pasta dish!

Tomato and Mozzarella Caprese

Ingredients:

- **4 large ripe tomatoes** (sliced into rounds)
- **8 ounces (225 grams) fresh mozzarella cheese** (sliced into rounds)
- **1/4 cup fresh basil leaves** (whole or roughly torn)
- **2 tablespoons extra-virgin olive oil**
- **1 tablespoon balsamic vinegar** (optional, for a tangy touch)
- **Salt and pepper** to taste
- **1/2 teaspoon sea salt** (optional, for finishing)
- **1/4 teaspoon crushed red pepper flakes** (optional, for a bit of heat)

Instructions:

1. **Arrange the Salad:**
   - On a large serving platter or individual plates, alternate and overlap the tomato slices and mozzarella slices in a circular pattern or in rows.
2. **Add the Basil:**
   - Tuck whole or torn basil leaves between the slices of tomato and mozzarella.
3. **Drizzle with Oil and Vinegar:**
   - Drizzle the extra-virgin olive oil evenly over the salad.
   - If using, drizzle with balsamic vinegar for added flavor.
4. **Season the Salad:**
   - Season with salt and pepper to taste.
   - Optionally, sprinkle with sea salt for a finishing touch and add crushed red pepper flakes if you like a bit of heat.
5. **Serve:**
   - Serve immediately at room temperature.

Tips:

- **Use Fresh Ingredients:** The quality of the tomatoes and mozzarella will greatly impact the flavor of the dish.
- **Try Different Varieties:** For a colorful presentation, you can use heirloom tomatoes or a mix of cherry tomatoes.
- **Make Ahead:** If preparing in advance, assemble the salad without the olive oil and vinegar, and add them just before serving to avoid sogginess.

Tomato and mozzarella Caprese is a timeless dish that's perfect as a starter or a side. Its simplicity allows the fresh flavors to shine, making it a favorite for any occasion. Enjoy!

Chilled Beet Soup

Ingredients:

- **4 medium beets** (peeled and diced)
- **1 small onion** (chopped)
- **2 cloves garlic** (minced)
- **1 tablespoon olive oil**
- **4 cups vegetable broth** (or chicken broth)
- **1 medium potato** (peeled and diced)
- **1 tablespoon red wine vinegar** (or apple cider vinegar)
- **1 teaspoon sugar** (optional, to balance the flavors)
- **Salt and pepper** to taste
- **1/2 cup sour cream** (or Greek yogurt, for creaminess)
- **2 tablespoons fresh dill** (chopped, for garnish)
- **1 tablespoon fresh chives** (chopped, for garnish, optional)

Instructions:

1. **Cook the Beets:**
   - In a large pot, heat the olive oil over medium heat.
   - Add the chopped onion and cook until softened and translucent, about 5 minutes.
   - Add the minced garlic and cook for another 1-2 minutes until fragrant.
2. **Add the Beets and Potato:**
   - Stir in the diced beets and potato.
   - Pour in the vegetable broth and bring to a boil.
   - Reduce the heat to a simmer and cook for about 20-25 minutes, or until the beets and potatoes are tender.
3. **Blend the Soup:**
   - Allow the soup to cool slightly. Use an immersion blender to puree the soup until smooth. Alternatively, you can transfer the soup in batches to a blender. Be careful with hot liquids.
   - Once blended, return the soup to the pot if you used a blender.
4. **Season and Chill:**
   - Stir in the red wine vinegar and sugar (if using).
   - Season with salt and pepper to taste.
   - Let the soup cool to room temperature, then refrigerate for at least 2 hours, or until well chilled.
5. **Serve:**
   - Ladle the chilled beet soup into bowls.
   - Swirl a dollop of sour cream or Greek yogurt into each bowl.
   - Garnish with fresh dill and chives, if desired.

Tips:

- **Adjust the Consistency:** If the soup is too thick after blending, you can thin it out with a bit more vegetable broth or water.
- **Add Toppings:** Besides sour cream, you can also top with croutons or a sprinkle of extra fresh herbs for added texture and flavor.
- **Make Ahead:** This soup can be made a day or two in advance and stored in the refrigerator. The flavors often improve after a day.

Chilled beet soup is a unique and refreshing option for summer meals, combining earthy beet flavor with a cool, creamy texture. Enjoy!

Grilled Portobello Mushrooms with Balsamic Glaze

Ingredients:

- **4 large Portobello mushrooms** (stems removed and cleaned)
- **1/4 cup extra-virgin olive oil**
- **2 tablespoons balsamic vinegar**
- **2 cloves garlic** (minced)
- **1 teaspoon dried oregano** (optional)
- **1 teaspoon dried thyme** (optional)
- **Salt and pepper** to taste
- **1/4 cup balsamic glaze** (store-bought or homemade, see note below)
- **Fresh parsley** (chopped, for garnish, optional)

Instructions:

1. **Prepare the Marinade:**
   - In a small bowl, whisk together the olive oil, balsamic vinegar, minced garlic, dried oregano, and dried thyme (if using).
   - Season with salt and pepper to taste.
2. **Marinate the Mushrooms:**
   - Brush the Portobello mushrooms with the marinade on both sides.
   - Let them marinate for at least 15-30 minutes. For more flavor, you can marinate them for up to 2 hours in the refrigerator.
3. **Preheat the Grill:**
   - Preheat your grill to medium-high heat.
4. **Grill the Mushrooms:**
   - Place the marinated mushrooms on the grill, gill side down.
   - Grill for about 5-7 minutes per side, or until the mushrooms are tender and have nice grill marks. Baste with additional marinade during grilling if desired.
5. **Apply the Balsamic Glaze:**
   - Remove the mushrooms from the grill and drizzle with balsamic glaze.
6. **Garnish and Serve:**
   - Garnish with chopped fresh parsley if desired.
   - Serve warm as a main dish or a side.

Homemade Balsamic Glaze (Optional):

If you prefer to make your own balsamic glaze, here's a quick recipe:

Ingredients:

- **1 cup balsamic vinegar**
- **2 tablespoons honey** (or maple syrup)

Instructions:

1. **Reduce the Balsamic Vinegar:**
    - In a small saucepan, combine the balsamic vinegar and honey.
    - Bring to a boil, then reduce the heat and simmer for about 10-15 minutes, or until the mixture has reduced by half and has a syrupy consistency.
    - Allow to cool before using.

This recipe for grilled Portobello mushrooms with balsamic glaze is a fantastic way to enjoy the rich, umami flavor of Portobellos enhanced by a tangy-sweet glaze. It's perfect for a summer BBQ or as a standout vegetarian dish. Enjoy!

Herb-Roasted Chicken with Root Vegetables

Ingredients:

For the Chicken:

- **1 whole chicken** (about 4-5 pounds)
- **2 tablespoons olive oil**
- **2 tablespoons fresh rosemary** (chopped, or 2 teaspoons dried rosemary)
- **2 tablespoons fresh thyme** (chopped, or 2 teaspoons dried thyme)
- **4 cloves garlic** (minced)
- **1 lemon** (cut into wedges)
- **Salt and pepper** to taste

For the Vegetables:

- **4 medium carrots** (peeled and cut into chunks)
- **3-4 medium parsnips** (peeled and cut into chunks)
- **2 medium potatoes** (peeled and cut into chunks)
- **1 large onion** (cut into wedges)
- **2 tablespoons olive oil**
- **1 teaspoon dried rosemary** (or 1 tablespoon fresh rosemary)
- **1 teaspoon dried thyme** (or 1 tablespoon fresh thyme)
- **Salt and pepper** to taste

Instructions:

1. **Preheat Oven:**
   - Preheat your oven to 425°F (220°C).
2. **Prepare the Chicken:**
   - Pat the chicken dry with paper towels.
   - Rub the chicken all over with olive oil.
   - Season generously with salt and pepper.
   - Rub the minced garlic, chopped rosemary, and thyme all over the chicken.
   - Place lemon wedges inside the cavity of the chicken.
3. **Prepare the Vegetables:**
   - In a large bowl, toss the carrots, parsnips, potatoes, and onion with olive oil, dried rosemary, dried thyme, salt, and pepper.
4. **Arrange the Chicken and Vegetables:**
   - Place the seasoned vegetables in the bottom of a large roasting pan.
   - Place the chicken on top of the vegetables. This allows the vegetables to cook in the chicken juices, adding extra flavor.
5. **Roast the Chicken and Vegetables:**

- Roast in the preheated oven for about 1.5 to 2 hours, or until the chicken reaches an internal temperature of 165°F (74°C) in the thickest part of the thigh, and the vegetables are tender.
- Baste the chicken with its juices halfway through the roasting time. If the vegetables are browning too quickly, cover them loosely with foil.

6. **Rest the Chicken:**
   - Once the chicken is done, remove it from the oven and let it rest for about 10-15 minutes before carving. This allows the juices to redistribute and ensures a moist chicken.
7. **Serve:**
   - Carve the chicken and serve with the roasted root vegetables.

Tips:

- **Use Fresh Herbs:** Fresh herbs provide a more vibrant flavor, but dried herbs work well too if fresh isn't available.
- **Add Variety:** You can also include other root vegetables like sweet potatoes or turnips for added variety.
- **Make It a Meal:** This dish pairs well with a simple green salad or some crusty bread.

Herb-roasted chicken with root vegetables is a classic and comforting meal that's both easy to prepare and delicious. Enjoy your wholesome, hearty dinner!

www.ingramcontent.com/pod-product-compliance
Lightning Source LLC
LaVergne TN
LVHW081614060526
838201LV00054B/2250